The New English Garden

Photographs by Andrew Lawson

with Jane Sebire and Rachel Warne

F

FRANCES LINCOLN LIMITED
PUBLISHERS

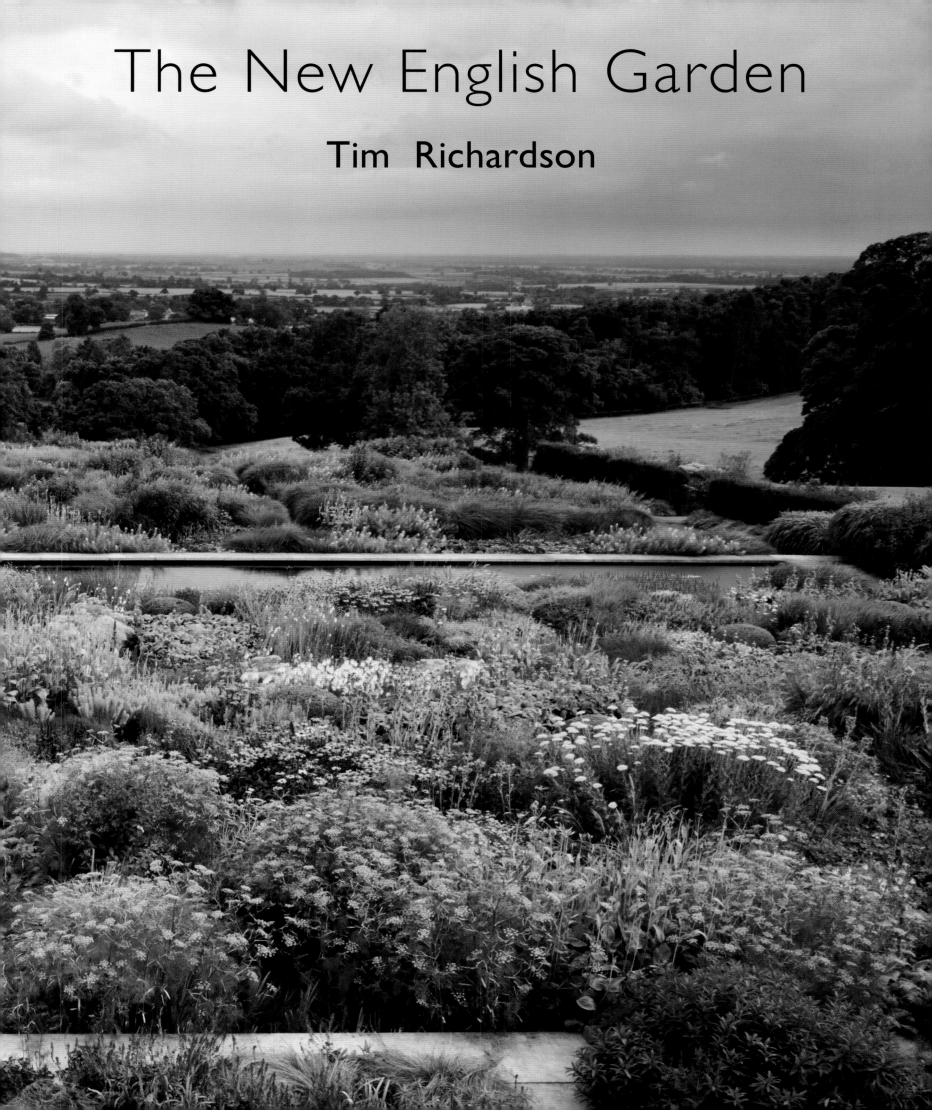

The New English Garden

Tim Richardson

Contents

Frances Lincoln Limited
www.franceslincoln.com

The New English Garden
Copyright © Frances Lincoln Limited 2013
Text copyright © Tim Richardson 2013
Photographs copyright © Andrew Lawson 2013
Pages 34–35, 50–63, 170–181, 234–243, 280, 282–285
copyright © Jane Sebire
Pages 9, 136–145, 162–169, 200–209, 258–271, 286–291
copyright © Rachel Warne
Page 281 copyright © Arabella Lennox-Boyd

First Frances Lincoln edition 2013

Tim Richardson has asserted his right to be identified
as the author of this work in accordance with the
Copyright, Designs and Patents Act 1988 (UK)

A catalogue record for this book is available from the
British Library.

ISBN 978-0-7112-3270-9

Designed by Anne Wilson
Printed and bound in China

9 8 7 6 5 4 3 2

HALF-TITLE PAGE A padlock at Plaz Metaxu
TITLE PAGE Large-scale plantings at Mount St John

Introduction

The 'new' English garden?

That's a big claim. The sceptical reader may well ask: 'How can a well-known garden such as Great Dixter, or Trentham, or Highgrove, be described as "new"?'

When I started to consider which gardens should be included in this book, I decided that the most useful, and certainly the most interesting, way to proceed would be to concentrate on innovative gardens that have been made or remade during the past decade. They do not have to be gardens that have recently been created from scratch. Gardens of character do not generally emerge overnight: garden-making is a pursuit in which change and regeneration are natural and desirable, where the passage of time has a creative impact on the look and feel of the place. For a truly 'new' garden to bed down, for the plantings to mature and the hard materials to weather, can easily take a decade or more – sometimes much more: many landscape gardens are at their best when the trees have matured, perhaps 150 years after they were first laid out. At the same time, it is also possible to make something genuinely new on old soil. A new garden can be born of an old one, retaining part of an older identity while developing a new character. It is the relationship of a child to a parent, a chip off the old block, where the fads and foibles of successive generations can be traced in the visible and invisible fabric of the place. As Sylvia Crowe pointed out more than half a century ago, garden-making is all about process, not product.

For time is the essence of garden-making as a creative endeavour: a garden is forever changing, and on every scale of time – through the passage of centuries, years, seasons, days, hours, or even across a single minute. Garden-makers must accept – ideally with a sense of joy rather than trepidation – that their endeavours will always be subject to compulsory collaboration with the vagaries of conditions, and especially of the weather. Gardens could be said to present new versions of themselves on each successive day, and the look of a garden on a specific date one year may be quite different from the way it appears on the same date the following year. All that is before we even get on to the knotty issue of how they may be received in the minds and imaginations of multiple onlookers.

This kind of talk will irritate those who fear that gardens are getting above themselves. That is because the result of creative endeavours in other artistic and design disciplines tends to be object-based. A building stands there more or less immutable (if rarely inviolate). A picture or sculpture sits in the gallery or great house, where it can be approached, circled and venerated. These objects of cultural production have a tangible market value – and can in most cases be bought and sold readily enough. Gardens are different. They operate on another plane, with human interventions always subject to serious modification. This militates against the belief cherished in traditional art circles that the object produced somehow represents the unmediated imagination of the artist, who is responsible for every nuance, every mark. This notion does not last long in the garden setting, where trees die, rivers flood, unwanted weeds prevail and expensive plantings fail. Because of this gardens tend to inspire both fear and condescension in the cognoscenti of other disciplines, who often prefer to denigrate the garden as an outdoor version of DIY, a hobbyists' paradise or a rather too technical practice which is best avoided or sidelined. Gardens bust the boundaries of art, science, craft and hobbydom (as well as social class, on occasion), often to the chagrin of the guardians of those particular bailiwicks. The irony is that increasingly these other art

A quiet moment at a garden of strong symbolic inference: Plaz Metaxu in mid-Devon.

forms and genres have begun to reflect the cultural craving for a more meaningful relationship with the planet, placing an environmental or ecological understanding of the world at the heart of creative thinking. Increasingly, too, artworks are being conceived as processes or projects – though in most cases the artist still must reign as the Svengali of the piece. Nowadays, when people ask whether gardens can legitimately be considered as an art form, my riposte is that art should surely aspire to the condition of the garden.

But to return to the 'newness', or otherwise, of the gardens in this book.

An attempt has been made to present a wide selection of gardens which represent the contemporary scene. But one general theme does come through: flicking through the pages it becomes apparent that the trend over the past few decades has been towards a more naturalistic approach to garden-making. The background to this is elaborated in individual chapters, but a precis follows here.

By the early 1990s garden-making in Britain had reached the apotheosis of Arts and Crafts colour-theming, a rococo moment in which herbaceous borders had become extremely rich and complex in terms of the variety of plant material involved and the intricacy, subtlety and complexity of plant combinations selected for colour, form and texture. In design terms, it was almost as if the herbaceous border had nowhere else to go. This is not the place to go into the history of twentieth-century English planting design (a few years ago I attempted to trace this in a book entitled *English Gardens in the Twentieth Century*); suffice to say that the 1990s marked the end of a floriferous road which had been developing since the late Victorian period.

At this time, forward-looking garden-makers started to take more notice of the simpler approach to horticulture deployed in public parks in Germany (where Karl Foerster had had a great influence in the post-war period) and in the work of a group of nurserymen from Holland led by Piet Oudolf. A seminal conference held at Kew in 1994 brought together British designers who were – in retrospect – looking for a way out of the cul-de-sac represented by Arts and Crafts and the tradition of colour-theming borders in an episodic manner. A new palette of repeated grasses and large drifts of perennials (frequently tall or daisy-flowered) began to have an influence, in a movement initially known as the 'Dutch Wave', occasionally as 'matrix planting' but later more commonly as 'New Perennials'.

The majority of British designers (though not all: see Rupert Golby and George Carter, for example) have allowed themselves to be influenced by the New Perennials influx, the top designers absorbing such ideas into their own practice, creating gardens with a distinctive and individual look as opposed to mere replicas of a European import. The British context must also be taken into account here, with Beth Chatto in particular creating a beacon of innovative planting style and a more relaxed attitude to planting complexity at her garden in Essex (the work of Dan Pearson, for example, is better understood in that context).

The high watermark of the New Perennials-inspired naturalistic planting movement in Britain might be considered to be Trentham, which includes the work of both Oudolf and Tom Stuart-Smith (whose practice is inflected by New Perennials but retains a deal of 'English' complexity and emotional engagement); or Waltham Place, where Henk Gerritsen, another Dutch gardener, took naturalistic planting to an extreme. Worldwide it has to be the High Line linear park in Manhattan, where Oudolf created a series of linked plantings. More recently, the naturalistic turn has possibly reached an apotheosis with the work of the Sheffield School, who created the wildflower meadows for the London 2012 Olympic Park, characterized as habitat replications rather than designed landscapes. It now feels as if the pendulum is swinging back towards a more traditional English model, with shrubs (roses leading the fragrant charge) making their way back into borders, and a slightly more intricate planting regimen (though nothing as fully worked as the 'tapestry' look of yore) being introduced. This is a style which has been in abeyance but not in stasis: while everyone's focus has been on swaying clumps of grasses, surging foxtail lilies and phlomis, and banks of echinaceas, heleniums and rudbeckias, under the radar 'traditional' English garden style has been quietly developing.

In any case the naturalistic turn in English planting, and the beginnings of a reaction to it, do not constitute the whole story. This book contains a number of gardens which illustrate other aspects of the contemporary scene, from the formal tradition (Tilbury) to the potager (Daylesford), the eclectic garden (Highgrove), conceptualism (Angel Field), living walls (Athenaeum Hotel), modernism (Bury Court), abstract turf landforming (Ascott), historicism (Hanham

Court), autobiography (The Laskett), science (Througham Court), plantsmanship (Great Dixter) and the symbolic landscape garden (Plaz Metaxu). On this evidence there is no danger of English gardens becoming stereotypical or stuck in a rut.

English gardens are at an exciting and fruitful juncture. The level of horticultural and aesthetic sophistication in garden-making has not been so high since the early eighteenth century. It will come as no surprise when matters continue to develop apace. I can think of at least five gardens which are already moving the story along, though they are too young and unformed to be included in this book.

But, as authors often say at the end of a book introduction: watch this space.

Naturalistic gardening to the max in Henk Gerritsen's planting at Waltham Place in Berkshire.

Armscote Manor

Dan Pearson

Dan Pearson's signature plantings of eremurus (foxtail lilies) mingle with *Salix exigua* at Armscote Manor.

Immaculately clipped box hedges and trained fruit trees are features of the kitchen garden at this compact estate.

DAN PEARSON is a designer who has travelled a long way, stylistically, in the course of a career which began in the early 1990s, when most British garden designers remained entranced by Arts and Crafts traditions of herbaceous planting which dated back almost a century. At this time Dan was almost alone in advocating a more modern solution for modern garden situations. In a string of private gardens, and via a succession of television series in the 1990s, he promoted the idea of a garden which united a love of plants and the natural world with a kind of stylish functionalism that strongly appealed to younger garden owners.

By the late 1990s this approach and attitude had gone mainstream, and Dan was rightly hailed as an innovator who had been ahead of his time. If anything, however, his work has become more naturalistic over the years, testament to his serious credentials as a plantsman, with a Kew training and years of experience with plant communities in the wild all over the world. One of his formative influences as a gardener was Beth Chatto, whose garden in Essex demonstrates the way a garden's style can reflect the habits of self-supporting communities of plants as they thrive in nature. To this Dan adds a deep appreciation of a site's sense of place, which he aims to enhance and reflect with his designs. Recently his practice has expanded internationally, with projects in Italy, the USA and Japan, where he is collaborating with Conran & Partners in creating fourteen ambitious roof gardens for the Roppongi Hills housing development in Tokyo, and he has done important work in the Millennium Forest on the north island of Hokkaido, where his wildflower meadows and landforms are part of an overall strategy devised by the Japanese designer Takano.

Dan's gardens are usually based on strong, clear structural bones, in terms both of sinuous, elegant curves in the hard landscape and ground plan, and of horticultural features such as lines of pleached trees, or clipped yew hedges in bulbous form. A sculpted spatial quality resonates through the work. In recent commissions Dan has explored an ever more naturalistic feel, with an emphasis on wildflower plantings with mown paths meandering through them, plantings of native trees, subtle turf landforms and the decorative possibilities of walling based on traditional styles. Decorative plantings near buildings often give way to plantings of native species at the boundaries of the garden. At his most significant long-term project, Home Farm in Northamptonshire (where he worked for fourteen years), it was the surrounding agricultural landscape of ancient ridge-and-furrow fields which provided the inspiration. But there is always room for decorative expression: in a sun trap close to a converted barn at Home Farm, Dan created an exuberant garden of hot colours: kniphofias, achilleas, crocosmia and his signature plant, eremurus (the soaring foxtail lily).

That garden (now in new hands and somewhat altered) was celebrated in a book and a television series, but another long-term project started early in his career (1995), Armscote Manor in Warwickshire, has received far less attention. At this garden, Dan's understanding of the way spatial design can be melded with naturalistic planting is displayed to equally good effect. In a series of hedged and walled enclosures around a Jacobean manor house, Dan has played with ideas of formality and informality by clipping topiary into vegetable shapes and creating a vibrant hot border of oranges and reds right next door to an elegant garden of silvers and whites, bordered by yew hedges and a pleached hornbeam walk. There is a formal canal, a nuttery, an arboretum of native British trees, and a 'wind garden' of plants and trees that move and rustle in the breeze. This is essentially a garden of dichotomies – between hot and cold colours, rough and smooth, open and enclosed, straight and wavy.

In some ways this is a classic English manor house and garden, with that familiar garden-room layout of hedged and walled enclosures, a 1920s sunken Italianate pool garden, and a straight path to the front door flanked by vibrant lavender and four ancient yew topiaries. But Pearson (while acknowledging Hidcote as an inspiration) has treated each space with individuality and flair. The entrance to the property heralds its modern credentials. The visitor approaches the house along a winding drive through a small park of mature chestnuts and limes, where a herd of pedigree Portland sheep grazes. So far, so conventionally pleasing. But approaching from the service areas to the east, one finds the entrance to the house prefaced by a modernistic, abstracted arrangement of tightly clipped hornbeam islands, sprouting from large cushions of yew hedging, all set in a sea of grey gravel. Four flat-topped yew obelisks underplanted with white lavender are another statement of intent. These features set up an expectation in the visitor that this garden will be directive

in its planting aesthetic, that there will be unfamiliar plantings and perhaps some challenging moments.

This eastern 'side' entrance is used as the front door by the owners, and is reached via a small enclosed courtyard. The official front of the house, to the south, has the long straight path to the front door, flanked by large lawns bounded by walls. The beds along the house frontage contain an exuberant summer mix of black and red hollyhocks, with gypsophila, santolina, poppies, foxgloves and phlox. The look is pretty but not frothy. Another interesting note is created by the yew hedging against the walls of this front garden area, to the west of the house front. These have been clipped into sinuous, wavy shapes which add a touch of modernistic elegance to the scene and contrast with fluffy beds of *Alchemilla mollis* below.

An entrance on the north side of the space leads directly into the sunken pool garden, where all roads at Armscote seem to lead. This is the most architecturally interesting space in the garden, with a wide terrace on the southern and eastern (house) sides. The pool garden is now characterized as a rose garden, with large

Visitors to the house approach via a series of intriguing modernist digressions including 'islands' of clipped hornbeams arising from cushions of clipped box (opposite). At the front of the house is a conventional lawn with an Arts and Crafts corner pavilion (above), given a modern appeal by simple fringe plantings of *Alchemilla mollis* and a distinctive wavy-topped hedge.

The most richly ornamented space, and perhaps the heart of the garden, is the sunken Italianate pool garden, where shaggy *Rosa rugosa* bushes contrast with the rigour of clipped box balls and a dignified, shady catalpa on the terrace at its head.

specimens of *Rosa rugosa* treated almost as a hedge plant, supplemented by varieties such as 'Roseraie de l'Häy'. But the most striking design element is the treatment of the evergreens, which are tightly clipped but arranged in groups of balls or as skirts to trees (such as shady catalpa) in a wholly asymmetrical and seemingly random manner. The result is a pleasing contrast between riotous rose bushes and coolly sculpted hedging. The roses are bolstered by mulleins in purple and white (a theme throughout the garden), white lavenders and little erigeron daisies, with frothy hydrangeas adding bulk near the house.

The western part of the garden is taken up by a succession of connected garden spaces which are all quite different. From the immaculate small walled kitchen garden at the south-west, replete with espaliers and fruit cage, plus some unusual clipped yew forms in the cruciform layout of beds, one proceeds to a double herbaceous border which was orginally conceived as 'hot' (part of that Hidcote influence). It is now more varied, with 1990s stalwarts such as *Crocosmia* 'Lucifer', *Knautia macedonica*, alliums and the red *Achillea* 'Walther Funcke' relieved by the

BELOW The hot borders at Armscote (with crocosmia in the foreground) create a fiery contrast with the cool restraint which reigns in most of the rest of the garden.

OPPOSITE A Chinese-style moon gate has been punched through the middle of one side of the walled garden, connecting it with the more decorative areas beyond.

more naturalistic influence of verbascums (especially *V. chaixii*), massed daylilies and bronze fennel.

The largest horticultual display space flanks a pleached hornbeam walk that extends west from the sunken garden. The small willow *Salix exigua* is used (unusually) as a unifying device, along with silvery artemisia, providing an intriguing backdrop to spiky eryngiums and a variety of soft grasses, plus outbursts of eremurus here and there. A short canal extends laterally from one side of the hornbeam walk, while a long border of iris has its season extended by means of that complex and characterful onion *Allium cristophii*.

A pleached hornbeam walk extends from the sunken garden, flanked by a wide border of vibrant perennials and sculptural grasses, and backed by the distinctive green of the small willow *Salix exigua*.

The northern part of the garden, overlooking the park, has recently been given a meadow feel, with stipa and deschampsia grasses given late summer zip by helenium and rudbeckia flowers, the design focused on a small wooden summerhouse with conical roof. But once again here Pearson does not allow the garden spaces to relax into themselves too much for their own good, for he has interpolated a rigorous formal device in the form of a grid of willow trees, which add a felicitous note of formality, answering the subtle grandeur of the park views – here again there is a strong savour of Hidcote, as there is in

the general rhythm of long, corridor-like vistas alternating with small enclosed areas in the garden proper.

The garden at Armscote is a highly complex design of many elements, offering a sense of variation within unity. It is like a tasting menu in a restaurant, where all the elements combine to create a sense of a signature style.

At the farther reaches of the ornamental part of the garden, Pearson has introduced a meadow feel by means of massed plantings of rudbeckia and stipa and deschampsia grasses around a conical-roofed pavilion, Adirondack chairs overlooking the ha-ha and a grid of willow trees.

Mount St John
Tom Stuart-Smith

PERHAPS MORE THAN any other garden designer working today, Tom Stuart-Smith has an outlook that results from an amalgam of two major influences. The first is traditional British border design: the intensely decorative, colour-themed, 'tapestry' tradition which takes the herbaceous border as its touchstone and has elements of cottage gardening as well as more prescriptive ideas derived from the early twentieth-century writings of Gertrude Jekyll and William Robinson. The second reflects the influx of new ideas about naturalistic planting which have been imported from the Netherlands and Germany since the mid-1990s, broadly categorized as the 'New Perennials' movement in planting design – all those grasses and 'drifts', designed to look almost as good in autumn and winter as in late summer, their climactic moment.

Stuart-Smith's response is the formulation of an idea of a continuum through the designed area: a garden which ebbs and flows with the seasons, without the use of specific highlights or designed episodes. This attitude stands in opposition to traditional colour-theming, which is carefully organized so that the mood of the border or overall garden can be felt to change decisively as one moves through it. For Stuart-Smith, a Beethoven enthusiast, a musical analogy is most fitting, in that themes can be reprised across a large area by means of repeat plantings of a small number of key plants which can be seen to ribbon through the space, producing highlights of intense colour and activity within a coherent whole. An analogy from the visual arts might suit equally well, in that traditional border design might be understood as 'figurative', while this new look could be dubbed 'abstract'.

'I never think of these spaces as rooms – I like everything to interconnect,' he explains. 'One overall story, with a series of subplots, not a series of episodes. I want the whole garden to be one malleable entity.' The designer's intention

OPPOSITE There are fine views across the Vale of York from the Palladian mansion at Mount St John.

ABOVE The terraced garden is divided into two sections: the one shown here is the more conventional space associated with the historic house.

BELOW A sandstone plinth
in a stylized grove at the top
of the 'modern' terrace acts
as an informal seat and helps
bring together the garden's
hard structural elements, so
they are not overwhelmed by
the massed plantings.
OPPOSITE Spikes of foxtail
lilies, salvias and rudbeckias
glimpsed through a gate, one
of the lateral views which
are important in this garden,
which is designed of course to
'be in' as well as be gazed at
from above.

is to deconstruct the elements of the garden until what is left is a central horticultural theme or tone, extrapolated evenly throughout.

Stuart-Smith, like many others, began his gardening career in thrall to the greats such as Sissinghurst and Hidcote. However, he has gradually cast off that sense of tradition – having gone through what he calls 'a fluffy pink stage' and 'something of an orange kniphofia moment'. Indeed, some traditionalists might be alarmed to hear his revelation that today 'grasses make up about 25 per cent of all the planting' in his own garden in Hertfordshire and that 'there is now not a single kniphofia or an old-fashioned rose or a delphinium.' Stuart-Smith tells how one American visitor reacted to his enthusiastic deployment of tall mulleins and Scotch thistle by exclaiming: 'Tom, your garden is so aggressive!'

Also intriguing is his theory around what he calls 'supernormal gardening', a term borrowed from zoology (Stuart-Smith's first degree) and used here to refer to naturalistic planting which evokes 'a sense of the confusingly semi-familiar' – an almost primal understanding of the look and feel of nature in the raw, which somehow relates to the genetic memory of *Homo sapiens*. This is a designer who is all too aware of the emotional effects of his garden designs, an aspect which many professionals are reluctant to acknowledge. As a trained landscape architect, he is also alive to the position of the garden in the wider landscape, remarking: 'In recent years I have come to see the garden less as a series of

events and more as part of a place in the landscape, an intermediary between the house and the wider setting.'

This sensibility is well illustrated by an ambitious recent project, the terraced garden at Mount St John in North Yorkshire, where an elegant small Palladian mansion of 1720 stands on the site of a monastery belonging to the Knights Hospitaller first recorded in 1017. The owners, the Blundell family, engaged Stuart-Smith in 2005 to create a garden on the steep slopes to the south of the house, which benefit from panoramic views across the rolling countryside of the Vale of York, to Sutton Bank in the distance and even, on a clear day, to York Minster.

A new wing in sympathetic if forgettable modern style had been added to the east side of the original house, so Stuart-Smith was faced with the problem of a garden that responded to two different architectural facades. Looking out in the other direction, the challenge was to create something which would not be merely 'a doormat to the panorama', as he put it. The solution to the latter was found by means of the sheer scale of his plans – especially the width of the terraces; so spacious is the landscape canvas that one would never imagine at first glance that the terraces cover almost three acres. Some 32,000 perennial plants were used for their first season, in April 2006, and of course the floral arsenal is restocked each year. The response to the architectural conundrum was equally decisive, in that Stuart-Smith has simply segmented the terrace into two distinct areas, to suit the different moods of the buildings, with a tall yew hedge acting as a partition.

The highlight is undoubtedly the 'modern' terraces which fall away beneath the new building on the eastern side. Smooth buffed sandstone has been deployed to create a series of retaining walls and terraces that create large planting beds or zones, interrupted halfway down by a rectangular swimming pool and associated deck, which acts as an invitation to descend. Yellow *Phlomis russeliana* is the horticultural star of the garden, uniting all the terraces and as useful an actor in the winter months, with its seed heads, as in the summer. Broadly, the planting theme is of more decorative, delicate floral material on the upper terraces, giving way to bulkier, more rangy and even ragged subjects (including numerous grasses) lower down. Among Stuart-Smith's stated design beliefs are: 'The bigger the space, the simpler the effect should be; in smaller spaces you can afford something quite varied,' and 'the bigger

the effect, the more often it has to be repeated.' Both are maxims which he has followed in this garden.

At the top of the terraces, a complex mix of clipped box balls ministers to a congregation of *Knautia macedonica*, blue eryngiums, alliums (seed heads left *in situ* when the purple colour fades), purple sedums and blue salvias (mainly varieties of *Salvia* x *sylvestris* including 'Mainacht' and 'Blauhügel'). Further down the slope these are joined by more yellow in the form of the phlomis in large clumps, *Coreopsis verticillata* 'Zagreb' and flat-topped *Achillea* 'Moonshine' and *A. filipendulina* 'Cloth of Gold', as well as grasses including panicum and *Deschampsia cespitosa* 'Goldehänge', foxtail lilies (*Eremurus* 'Pinokkio') and the largest eryngiums, *E. yuccifolium* and *E. agavifolium*. The latter, with its large, teasel-like seed heads, is especially effective in winter. Drifts of echinaceas, as well as the salvias, offset the yellows with rich purples and blues. The result is big, bold and operatic in scale, with the visitor sitting by the pool experiencing the horticultural equivalent of a seat in the stalls at Covent Garden or Glyndebourne. The comparison even has a physical dimension, in that it is necessary to file along the tops of the sandstone retaining walls in order to get in among the planted spaces, much like filing down a row of seats at the theatre.

But the garden at Mount St John is not all about the proscenium-arch experience: one important structural element is the use of diagonal emphases, partly created by means of the large box balls which are dotted across the space. This picks up on the way the topography of the fields beyond the ha-ha at the bottom of the garden undulates from side to side in a pleasingly chaotic way, naturally animating the foreground in a manner which would have pleased Humphry Repton (and would have cost his client a great deal to reproduce artificially). The emphasis in the planting is also basically lateral in orientation, which again helps emplace the terraces, so that they can hold their own in the face of the marvellous, dominating view.

The more traditional terrace has quieter and more conventional charms, the two large lawns at the heart a welcome cool palate-cleanser following the rich fare adjacent. The steps and stonework are a great pleasure here, leading down to the lawned area above the ha-ha which terminates the terrace and creates an invigorating sense of being poised above the landscape. Stuart-Smith would like to see a belvedere created at its eastern end, but for now a

stopping point is provided by a wide, low-slung wooden bench enwrapped in the voluptuous embrace of a cloud-formed box hedge of complex character, at the east end of the ha-ha lawn. Just above is a neat little feature: a series of clipped beech 'tumps' (neither a tower nor a hump) that helps define the edge of the terrace and create a sense of balance, while also giving a point to the Long Walk which runs down this side of the garden, edged with hostas, euphorbias and hollies, with a group of *Cornus controversa* at the top end, set among masses of hellebores.

ABOVE Hummocks of clipped yew and box provide a sense of structure and lateral movement in the densely planted 'modern' terraces, with a rich mix of perennial plantings that use repetition to instil a strong sense of rhythm.

OVERLEAF Big-scale plantings which bulk up in late summer successfully complement the big views. Halfway down the slope a lateral pool breaks up the space and invites the visitor in.

There are several other noteworthy elements to this garden, including an immaculate kitchen garden and an interesting area of sculptural evergreen planting in a parking area on the north side of the house. The Valley Garden, a large ravine to the west of the terraces, has recently been cleared (of wild garlic, mainly) and its three connecting ponds de-silted and ornamentally planted with gunnera, rodgersia, lythrum and other such favourites. These ponds were probably stew-ponds, stocked with the freshwater fish that was such an important element of the medieval diet (and a staple on meatless Fridays, of course). The upper slopes have been transformed into a maple bank on the east side, with groups of rhododendrons, beech and sycamore to the west and masses of persicaria below, together with the toughest groundcovers, ivy and vinca. It will take a few years for this area to mature and to relax into itself, creating the desired mysteriously sequestered air. It will add another dimension to a signally demonstrative garden.

In winter-time the forms of elements such as the beech 'tumps' (halfway between a tower and a hump) come into their own, alongside cloud-pruned box shapes and the tall stalks of perennials left to stand as long as possible. The new ravine garden, made from a series of medieval stew-ponds, features tree ferns and plantings of maples and rhododendrons.

Packwood House
Mick Evans

GARDENERS at famous topiary gardens sometimes find themselves in a bit of a bind. Unless their idea of fabulous horticultural practice is simply keeping hedges alive and if possible pristine, then the fact that their garden is celebrated almost solely for its topiary can become a little wearying. The best head gardeners overcome the problem by introducing superlative horticulture, if they can, in other parts of the garden. This has been the case at Levens Hall in Cumbria over the years, at Great Dixter too of course (it's easy to forget that it was the hedge system created by Nathaniel Lloyd which first made the garden famous), and now Mick Evans, the National Trust's head gardener at Packwood House, is demonstrating how a garden's planting can vie with its historical features as a visitor draw. The hot borders he has created are widely admired for their verve and originality, a development of horticultural traditions built up within the garden as opposed to outside influences. The National Trust should also be given credit for trusting its head gardener to experiment horticulturally in the most high-profile parts of this garden.

Packwood is internationally famous for its more or less astonishing Sermon on the Mount garden of yew topiaries, which occupies the rising ground south of the sixteenth-century house and culminates in the Mount from which the sermon is preached to the Apostles and the Multitude below. We can be fairly certain that when this garden was planted out between 1650 and 1670 by lawyer John Fetherston, the idea that it might depict a biblical scene was nowhere in his mind. It probably began as a modest formal feature intended to update a medieval inheritance, the Mount, which Fetherston like many other estate owners before and since was loath to remove despite its old-fashionedness. Sometimes this reticence came about for dynastic reasons (a Mount was an ancient feature and therefore showed that the family were of ancient lineage)

but obviously it was also practical (who wants to move a Mount?). Over the years Packwood's yew trees have grown to enormous and venerable size, 'peopling' the space so that a fertile mind might imagine they were gathered around the base of the Mount, conceivably as if they were attentively listening to a certain sermon.

It is not difficult to guess the era in which this spurious religious overlay was introduced. The Victorians not only rebranded this formal yew garden as the Sermon on the Mount garden, but augmented it with more yew topiaries to form the 'Multitude'. Today, each of these fine specimens has its own character, some growing to 15 metres/50 feet in height and leaning or bulging as is normal among those of a certain age. To walk among these personalities is a

ABOVE The view of the striking trio of gables from across the lawn is now leavened by the addition of a double border, here with verbascums resplendent.

RIGHT The yew topiaries at Packwood, probably planted in the mid-seventeenth century, have grown to enormous size and have become known as 'The Sermon on the Mount'.

memorable experience, like attending some mesolithic cocktail party. As Geoffrey Jellicoe remarked: 'It has a worldliness combined with a curious vague, indefinable mysticism.' The narrative may be concocted, but the yews speak for themselves.

Mick Evans and his colleagues must clip these titans across three months of the year, partly with the aid of a lorry-mounted hoist. Recently their attention has also been directed to various other parts of the garden, including the rejuvenated kitchen garden and a new orchard. But our focus here is to be on the borders at Packwood, and especially those which flank the terrace walk which extends laterally across the front edge of the Sermon on the Mount garden. This raised walk, which is 40 metres/130 feet long by 1.5 metres/5 feet at its widest, was subject to the attentions of Graham Baron Ash, the owner of Packwood from 1905 who created much of what the visitor experiences today. A flight of brickwork steps flanked by stone piers leads up

to the terrace, each end terminating in a delightful brick pavilion of strong seventeenth-century character, celebrated by *Country Life* magazine in 1904 for their delightful mouldering antiquity and still a wonderful asset to the garden. Until quite recently this was a fairly standard hot border for late summer appeal, dominated by the expected thrusting kniphofias and obligatory *Crocosmia* 'Lucifer' – but also cooled down somewhat by the burgeoning blues of cranesbill geraniums, flappy-leaved hostas and other interpolators, whose incongruous presence in a hot border was perhaps akin to that of cucumber on a barbecue.

In recent years Mick Evans has hotted up the border to furnace level and got rid of virtually everything which might calm it down – there is nothing dainty or decorous about the result; it is all about verve and vivaciousness. A great mass and variety of flowering material is closely packed into these borders, so that the plants must thrust upwards and forwards if they are to gain light. It's a race to the top over

the months of late summer and early autumn. In terms of planting design, the idea is not to create a narrative sweep across the length of the borders in the Jekyllian Arts and Crafts tradition, but to instigate instead a changing tapestry of plants with many repetitions. The tone remains basically constant and is extrapolated throughout; the interest lies in the complexity of the dense plantings, and the apparently random ways in which the plants interact with each other. Borders here are not so much about long views, but are best apprehended visually at close range, so that the solo visitor (and you will always feel solo, on this narrow path) seems immersed within at all.

There are two basic dichotomies or contrasts across the terrace borders. The first concerns shape, in that the verticals of the likes of yellow *Verbascum bombyciferum*, dark purple *Atriplex hortensis* 'Rubra' and those kniphofias are played off against the saucer tops of yellow *Achillea filipendulina* 'Gold Plate' and the orange-red *A.* 'Walther

Funcke'. The second is a matter of colour, in that the hot shades of yellow sunflower *Helianthus salicifolius* and rudbeckias, plus the oranges of *Tithonia rotundifolia* 'Torch' and marigolds, are given a further power boost by the deep purples of – especially – the atriplex, *Canna indica* 'Purpurea', and lower down *Phormium* 'Bronze Baby' and purple-toned *Euphorbia mellifera*. The deep-red-leaved *Ricinus communis* 'Impala' is particularly effective when juxtaposed with daisy forms such as heleniums, a potentially violent clash which is somehow absorbed into the overall display – perhaps because it is repeated so often (the horticultural equivalent of 'if you keep saying it, it will become true'). The *Crocosmia* genus

OPPOSITE The purple-red fronds of *Persicaria amplexicaulis* 'Firetail' erupt through clematis flowers in the hot borders.
BELOW The yew topiaries provide a strong backdrop for the thrusting forms of verbascum, achillea and *Verbena bonariensis*.

continues to manifest itself biblically, not only in 'Lucifer' but also in 'Babylon' and 'Star of the East'.

Other plant choices are cleverly pointed, notably the use of the intergalactically shaped, purple-black aeoniums ('Zwartkop' a favourite) and certain dahlias including *D.* Bishop's Children, here with deep red blooms. These intense tones add body to the scene and stop it looking too fluffy and insubstantial; they bring it back down to earth – just a little. Some blues have even been allowed to gatecrash the party, in the form of *Salvia patens* in various guises, including 'Blue Angel' and 'Guanajuato'. The display is also extended from top to bottom with violas and tropaeolum, which demonstrate wildly from the lower slopes of the volcano. One has heard the term 'riot of colour' often enough in border descriptions; this border looks as if it might be about to start helping the police with its enquiries.

It is notable how individual gardens often have their own highly specific traditions, methods and aims, very often founded upon the ideas and aspirations of some long-dead but influential and respected owner or head gardener. Packwood's garden provides a good example of this in that Mick Evans has consciously taken inspiration from a tradition begun by Packwood head gardeners of earlier generations, who were evidently still being schooled in the tradition of that great Victorian gardening writer, John Claudius Loudon. His *Encyclopaedia of Gardening* (1822) is a massive work and had a huge influence in its many editions through the nineteenth century, despite a certain amount of hackwork and repetition. In section 6,111 of this work, Loudon enumerates the principles of flower gardening by dividing them into three main classes: mingled, select and changeable. The select garden refers to a garden focused on specific kinds of plants, the changeable garden is one primarily in pots, while the mingled is 'by far the most common' – what most domestic gardeners were aiming at.

LEFT Earlier in the season, red Oriental poppies and dusky irises provide the overture to the main summer show, with blue veronicas and irises zipping up the scene.

RIGHT The fine gate piers add a distinguished note to the riotous border where the yellows of achillea and coreopsis are offset by orange rudbeckia and red crocosmia.

OVERLEAF The hot borders span the terrace between two brick pavilions. They are anchored and given rhythm by the dark form of aeonium and the vivid red splashes of *Crocosmia* varieties, principally 'Lucifer'.

'The object in this [the mingled] class', Loudon states, 'is to mix the plants, as that every part of the garden may present a gay assemblage of flowers of different colours during the whole season.' He goes on to suggest that the gardener's selection can be done 'without much regard to variety of form or diversity of character . . . The great art, therefore, in this kind of flower-border, is to employ such plants as produce large heads, or masses of flowers; to plant an equal number of every colour; and such a variety in regard to time of flowering as may afford some of every colour in flower from February to October.' A detailed methodology ensues, revealing that in practice this was a highly systematized approach, with alternating flower colour and blooming period calculated so that the 'mingling', or tapestry effect, can be enjoyed unfailingly through the season. (I cannot resist Loudon's observation that the actress Mrs Siddons was emphatically not a fan of this kind of planting, preferring masses of single flowers – especially violas – in her garden on the Harrow Road in west London.)

Mick has taken this idea of repetition and long-season interest and interpreted it in terms of plant matrices which can be repeated many times over across the borders. It is both a delight and a relief that the result looks nothing like Loudon's 'mingled' style would have done, with its height gradations and obsessively systematic seasonal planting regimen. That would have looked far too buttoned-up for today's tastes. Visitors' expectations have to be reckoned

ABOVE Looking through colourful plantings of helenium, *Hemerocallis* 'Stafford' and red tufted monarda in the main border to the quieter dry garden.
RIGHT A long border against the high wall by the house now takes second place to the exuberant plantings on the terrace and on the lawn borders, but its cool yellow themes act as a sorbet after the fiery fare elsewhere.

with, as well as the realities of maintenance. Although it would have been an intriguing experiment, it is doubtful many gardeners today would be able to go against all of their instincts all of the time in maintaining a true 'mingled' border in nineteenth-century style.

So Mick has opted instead for a 'historical' style which is paradoxically acutely in tune with the current zeitgeist in planting, in that it is founded on repetition of key plants, with a strong emphasis on structure and form. This is well illustrated in the new borders (established in 2006) which now extend across the south lawn up to the base of the terrace walk, creating a vista towards the largest yew topiary – named, slightly sinisterly, 'The Master' – up and beyond it. The main colour tone is plum-

OPPOSITE Purple and blue salvias are a key element here, contrasting with the reds of sanguisorba and lychnis and the strident forms of the cardoon, *Cynara cardunculus*.
ABOVE The new summer borders stride across the lawn, with the grass *Stipa gigantea* planted at regular intervals along their length.

The sunken garden is a classic Arts and Crafts feature imaginatively reworked using a dry-garden palette planted in gravel. It makes for an unusual contrast: the cool pool and lush grass with raised beds of sun-loving flowers in bright tones.

purple and purple-red – from salvias of all sorts, as well as *Campanula takesimana* 'Elizabeth', cirsiums, knautias, alliums and pulmonarias – while the structural body is provided by the regular explosions along its length of the foliage effusions of *Yucca recurvifolia*, the big sprays of grass *Stipa gigantea* and that stately vegetable the cardoon (*Cynara cardunculus*). In terms of detail, connoisseurs' favourites such as *Cerinthe major* var. *purpurascens*, Siberian iris 'Silver Edge' and *Sanguisorba menziesii* can be enjoyed. It has to be said that this border does not look precisely like other fashionable plantings of our

age, in that the repetition is far more regular and visibly systematic – you can almost measure out your paces by the intervals between the stipa, for example. A border of such regular habits may not be to everyone's tastes, but it has the massive virtue of originality.

A sunken garden on the east side of the lawn is a remnant from Baron Ash's day, updated as a Mediterranean garden and picking up on the repeat theme of the plantings in the long borders nearby, though here the emphasis is on the likes of kniphofias, euphorbias, eryngiums, *Zauschneria* species and succulents such as *Echeveria*. Beyond are

roses planted in the bays and against the orange-red brick walls of this large enclosed area, red alternating with white in unselfconscious candy stripes. It's a sweet note to end on, in a garden of finely honed innovation and individuality.

Scampston Hall
Piet Oudolf

THE WALLED GARDEN at Scampston Hall, Yorkshire, opened in 2004, was Dutch planting designer Piet Oudolf's second major commission at a privately owned garden in Britain, following his debut at Bury Court (see page 286). Despite some structural shortcomings, it stands as one of the most interesting and ambitious gardens of the first decade of the twenty-first century.

The overall estate at Scampston is of considerable garden-historical interest, with a fine small park landscaped by 'Capability' Brown in 1773, the remains of earlier formal work by Charles Bridgeman dating from the 1720s and a pioneering rock garden created by W.H. St Quintin in 1890, which is undergoing continued restoration. Sir Charles Legard inherited Scampston in 1994 – the estate has been in his family since 1690 – and with his wife, Caroline, first set about putting the dilapidated house in order.

In 1998 the Legards attended a talk given by Oudolf at Bury Court, spoke to him afterwards and were won by his modesty and down-to-earth nature, as well as by his obvious talent as a horticultural designer, which was then just beginning to be acknowledged in Britain. They invited him up to Scampston to assess the capabilities of the 1.8-hectare/4½-acre walled garden, which had been given over entirely to Christmas tree production. The idea was to turn the walled garden into a visitor attraction, in the hope that it would help the estate pay its way.

LEFT At Scampston's walled garden, visitors first circumnavigate the central space along a heavily planted perimeter walkway and are then hit with this view of waving lines of molinia grass.
OVERLEAF The molinia has quite a different character in early summer, with a distinct two-tone coloration. The centre of the space is marked by a quartet of robinias.

ABOVE At the centre of the garden is a dipping pool with a fountain surrounded by four quarter beds containing Piet Oudolf's signature plantings of perennials and grasses, which continue to look good until the end of autumn, as the browns, russets and deep oranges take over and dead stems with seed heads are left to stand.

LEFT The Spring Box Garden consists of seven topiarized squares offset by grasses and perennials; its pendant is the Summer Box Garden, which runs parallel on the other side of the walled garden.

Oudolf saw past both the wood and the trees and, on the kitchen table at Scampston, immediately sketched out a basic design on a large sheet of paper. This spontaneous reaction provided the basis for what the walled garden was to become: an intense arrangement of eight heavily planted and topiarized compartments, with a long perimeter walkway around three sides of the rectangular space, which acts as an overture before the symphonic movements of the principal areas. The only major change to this initial plan was the later addition of a mount at the north-west corner.

For Oudolf, it was, then, almost a blank canvas, with ambitious and supportive clients to boot. The only elements of the existing walled garden which had to be retained were the eighteenth-century brick walls and a listed glasshouse halfway down the north side of the garden, facing south to catch the most of the sunshine; the glasshouse remains *in situ* in a semi-derelict state, awaiting restoration (plans are underway). The beech hedge system was planted in 1999 and, principally for financial reasons, a concerted effort was made to propagate all the necessary plants: 4,500 beech plants were needed, as well as many thousands of perennials and grasses. The garden opened to the public in 2004 and, although it has yet to mature, especially in the areas of topiary and hedging, it has proved a hit with visitors, who appreciate its zest and originality, as well as the star quality bestowed by Oudolf's involvement. At the moment Scampston's walled garden is like an unruly but charismatic teenager: half-formed, but an entity you sense could develop into something remarkable.

The main criterion for inclusion in this book, *The New English Garden*, is evidence of new thinking and new ideas. Scampston has this in spades. However – to get the criticism out of the way – the overall structure of the new walled garden is a failure. Oudolf's stated intention was to create a garden in the cellular, compartmentalized tradition of English Arts and Crafts gardens such as Sissinghurst, Hidcote and Rodmarton, but the garden he created at Scampston bears little resemblance to that tradition, where rhythm is so important. The error has been to cram the garden 'rooms' together, with no meaningful linking passages and no refreshing pauses between areas of intensity. To pursue the architectural analogy, the overall impression is not of a rambling manor house with doorways leading into intriguing rooms, but of a great hall which has been simplistically partitioned. The over-schematic and rather overbearing result brings to mind the German architectural term *Schwellenangst*, which describes the stress felt by the users of pre-eighteenth-century houses whose rooms gave directly on to each other, without the benefit of either a corridor or the neutral space created by halls and landings.

As an ex-nurseryman, Oudolf's great strength lies of course in planting design, and it is perhaps telling that as his career has developed he has undertaken less and less landscape design, usually coming in as a design partner once a structure has been decided upon, filling in the required spaces with planting schemes (the High Line in New York is a case in point).

Despite this criticism one has to admire the ambition and originality of Oudolf's structural plans at Scampston, including the decision to create the long Plantsman's Walk which visitors must travel from the entrance point, across the top (west) perimeter of the garden, all the way down the south side, and then halfway along the east side, where the entrance to the garden proper is situated. This walk is bounded on the inner side by a beech hedge topped by pleached limes, so that all the attention is on the long borders against the wall, bursting with unusual or interesting shrubs and perennials, many of them chosen for foliage effect (*Tetrapanax papyrifer*, for example, makes a big show) and multi-season qualities. Hydrangeas are a particular interest, with *H. arborescens* 'Annabelle' and a huge specimen of *H. heteromalla* Bretschneideri Group grabbing the attention. The overall feel is woodlandy, with unruly box, hostas, heucheras, arisaemas, all kinds of ferns, epimediums, hepaticas, various syringas and five species of *Tricyrtis* among the pleasures. There is flower colour from more than a dozen peony species (notably *Paeonia* Gansu Group), cranesbill geraniums, trilliums, daphnes and stand-out plants such as *Ligularia japonica* 'Rising Sun'. All these plants are labelled numerically and can be checked against a list which runs to almost 1,500 species and varieties.

The effect of this extremely long planted passageway is rather unrelenting, however, and in the end one is delighted to turn the corner into the first – and most immediately striking – of the eight hedged compartments in the garden proper. This is a grass garden of highly defined, sinuous drifts of a single cultivar – *Molinia caerulea* subsp. *caerulea* 'Poul Petersen' – which come into their own in late summer and autumn (but are likely to be somewhat underwhelming at other times, as is the way with grasses).

ABOVE In the Silent Garden sentinel yews with clipped plinth-like bases, looking rather like chessmen, surround a square pool. OVERLEAF Even in early winter the Katsura Grove is an interesting place to be. The deep purple tones of the sedum are lifted by the whitening inflorescences of the surrounding grasses, which really come into their own at this season and at this scale.

These drifts cut across a handsome brick path which leads to a central area with four large blocky oak seats shaded by robinia trees. It is dramatic, but one has the sense that the ensemble would work better if it could be viewed from above. At the edges of the garden, plantings of salvias, cotinus, alliums, roses and nepeta pick up on the purple-

red tones of the molinia's inflorescences – the planting is where the subtlety and delight of this garden lie.

To the left is the Silent Garden, a suitably contemplative space where pillars of yew on square clipped bases are rationally arranged like chess pieces around a square reflecting pool. When they reach the required height of 3 metres/10 feet they will be clipped flat on top and thereafter kept at that size. To the right of the grass garden is one of the most popular areas, a vegetable and cut flower garden, the latter consisting of twelve circular beds. Straight ahead, cutting across the Grass Garden and Silent Garden at a right angle, is the corridor-like Spring Box Garden.

This consists of seven squares of box with sunken centres, flanked by narrow borders with geraniums, sage, nepeta, daylilies (*Hemerocallis* 'Gentle Shepherd' and 'Joan Senior'), *Astrantia* 'Claret', *Sedum* 'Iceberg', cardoons and a smattering of grasses including *Stipa gigantea*.

The simple charms of *Amsonia tabernaemontana* var. *salicifolia*, a low-clumping perennial with willow-like leaves, can be found here and in various parts of the walled garden, including inside the pendant to the Spring Box Garden, the Summer Box Garden, which is on the far side of the walled garden. In the Summer Box Garden, the box shapes are reversed in that they have small domes as opposed to saucers on top. The associated herbaceous material is also more exuberant, featuring the questing purple heads of *Veronicastrum virginicum* in no fewer than three cultivars – 'Fascination', 'Roseum' and 'Temptation', the last dominating, as it might – phlox, heucheras, thalictrum, lots of eupatorium and the grass *Deschampsia cespitosa*.

Sandwiched between these two sculpted box gardens is the Perennial Meadow, which has to be considered the highlight of the entire ensemble. Here, in four quarters arranged around the circular dipping pool which lies at the heart of the walled garden, Oudolf has created a master class in planting for structure, using his favoured range of perennials and grasses. It look marvellous late in the year in the evening light, and the plants chosen thrive on Scampston's light and well-drained soil. Oudolf's signature planting style is often criticized for its limitations in terms of scale – essentially, it looks best and is easiest to handle across big spaces, and it is sometimes deemed pointless on a domestic scale. It may indeed be true that it would not be possible to make this style work on the scale of a small or medium-sized garden, but the large Perennial Meadow does show that it would be feasible in a big garden, since each of these four quarters has its own internal logic.

Given the restrictions of space, here, Oudolf has used a more clump-based as opposed to drifting approach to planting design (compare this with his work on a bigger scale at Trentham, page 170). The vivid purples of salvias (mainly), *Monarda* 'Scorpion', echinaceas and nepeta create the primary rhythm across all four quarters, with textural interest from the spires of *Perovskia* 'Blue Spire' and eryngiums (including the delicate *E.* × *tripartitum*). The fresh greens of the clumped grasses *Sesleria autumnalis*, *S. nitida*, *Deschampsia cespitosa* and *Panicum virgatum* 'Rehbraun'

break up the colour intensity, while *Achillea* 'Walther Funcke' and *A.* 'Summerwine' create bright points of orange and red. Yellow *Phlomis russeliana* and *Coreopsis verticillata* 'Moonbeam', together with brick-red *Sedum* 'Matrona' and crimson *Knautia macedonica*, add further enrichment. The Perennial Meadow eclipses everything else in Scampston's walled garden and makes the topiary sections seem positively anaemic.

Adjacent to the Perennial Meadow is the Katsura Grove, where groups of these handsome small trees are gathered around a central planting of grass *Molinia caerulea* subsp. *arundinacea* 'Transparent'. This looks particularly fine in the autumn, as the leaves turn, offsetting the grasses below. To the west, beyond the partition of the Summer Box Garden, are the final two compartments of the walled garden, the Serpentine Garden to the left and the Mount to the right. The former is another topiarized area with a maze-like feel: six serpentines of clipped yew contained by clover-shaped elements. It is a little chilly. The Mount, at just 3.5 metres/12 feet tall, is the one element in this garden which really ought to be removed: it is not tall enough to serve any purpose in providing an overview of the garden, and it is not attractive, despite its pleasant setting in the midst of an 'orchard' of *Prunus* × *yedoensis* underplanted with spring bulbs – crocuses, camassias, fritillaries.

Not everything about this garden works, but the ambition and originality make it noteworthy. It already has plenty of fans and the walled garden is sure to develop in interesting ways in the hands of its indefatigable owners. And, anyway, isn't it so much more interesting to visit a thought-provoking garden where a statement is being made, rather than a 'classic' English garden of herbaceous borders which is resting on its (Portugal) laurels?

RIGHT Phlomis, rudbeckias, sedums, perovskias – the plant palette is typically Oudolfian at Scampston, the plants deployed with his usual regard for weighting, rhythm and repetition. There is none of the 'mingling' one would find in a more traditional English tapestry or cottage border.

OVERLEAF In early summer the central Perennial Meadow begins to present its character for the year. The bright purples and lush greens of this period will soon give way to richer reds, russets, oranges and golds.

Daylesford House

Mary Keen
Rupert Golby

WITH ITS OWN SATELLITE SHOPS and cafés in central London, as well as a new store in Tokyo, Daylesford is now an international brand as well as a Gloucestershire garden. For the past thirty years Daylesford House has been the home of Sir Anthony and Lady Bamford. The organic produce on sale online and in the shops comes from Daylesford's 800-hectare/2,000-acre estate farm, which also boasts holiday lets, a spa and a 'farm school'. At the house itself it is the walled kitchen garden which is the focus of gardening activity: an immaculately presented display of fruit and vegetables underpinned by a strong design component, courtesy of the input of garden designers Mary Keen and latterly Rupert Golby.

But there is more to Daylesford than the kitchen garden. The wider landscape is mysterious, private and subdued. The garden as a whole is characterized by careful attention to detail, discrimination and exactitude, which are all noteworthy qualities of Rupert Golby, a designer who trained with that exacting taskmaster Rosemary Verey. He is unusual as a designer in that he has no website and no hunger for publicity – which of course gives him an under-the-radar mystique and a word-of-mouth client base which has recently spread much wider than his native north Cotswolds.

There are three principal areas to this garden: the walled garden, the woodland and lakes, and the areas around the house.

RIGHT The landscape at Daylesford, including its two lakes, was created around the time the house was remodelled, in the 1780s, in 'Indian' fashion for Warren Hastings, first governor-general of India.
OVERLEAF The productive walled garden is the jewel of Daylesford, functioning as a decorative potager and producing, with a jaunty air, a cornucopia of vegetables and – especially – fruit.

ABOVE Willow and hazel provide decorative height as well as a support for beans and sweet peas. Flowers for cutting are grown against the low box hedges.

LEFT Rupert Golby has elaborated on Mary Keen's original design, adding more topiary and intensifying the plantings,

RIGHT Pears – one of the delights of this garden – are grown on canopies supported by metal frames.

The walled garden is the tour de force. Irregular, almost triangular in shape, the red-brick walls were built in 1789 as part of extensive remodelling by Warren Hastings, who bought the estate in 1788 and died there in 1818. A complex ground plan, largely the creation of Mary Keen in the late 1980s, carves up the area into formal spaces, some of which are hedged, in the cellular tradition of early twentieth-century Arts and Crafts gardening. About half is given over to the vegetables, a quarter is orchard and a quarter is decorative. This treatment, something of a throwback to the 1980s potager craze, is quite a rare sight nowadays, and it has not only worn and weathered well but has been developed in interesting ways by Golby during his eighteen years' tenure as consultant.

There is a pleasantly jaunty feel to the walled garden, thanks to the topiarized yew pheasants and cockerels which pop up among the eight quartered sets of box-edged beds – each 4.5 × 4.5 metres/15 × 15 feet – that form a rectangular parterre, bisected by a tunnel framed by apples and roses. Over the years Golby has greatly increased the richness and complexity of the original plantings and also the amount of clipped and topiary box, yew and Portugal laurel (the latter cut into eighteenth-century 'umbrello' forms). A careful and unegotistical designer, by his own account he has embellished and refined Mary Keen's work rather

than swept it away (something designers have a tendency to do with inherited projects). More recent additions are the woven willow and hazel structures which appear above the low box hedging around the beds; woven *in situ* in March, hazel is used for the uprights and willow for the whippy horizontals. Sweet peas and other old-fashioned flowers – especially roses, phlox and clematis – are planted up and around them, and they also provide support for gourds, marrows and beans. In late summer the sweet peas are removed from the structures, to be replaced by *Cobaea scandens* f. *alba*. Golby says that circular, vertical-sided cylinders have proven to be the most successful shape; the more traditional wigwams can cramp growth. Wide paths lined with Breedon grit traverse the vegetable parterre, the central walk lined by flower canals of cornflowers, *Echium vulgare* 'Blue Bedder', clary sage, nigella, *Papaver rhoeas* and *Scabiosa atropurpurea* 'Chile Black' – all used as valuable pollinators as well as for cutting.

The topiaries, woven cages and other decorative elements make the walled garden look like a garden first and a kitchen garden second; an ornamental, designed space which happens also to produce lots of different good things to eat. It's a fantasy garden, yes – but all run on strict organic lines and on rigorous principles of crop rotation. Golby explains how the cropping plan

for individual beds changes each year: radiating lines of alternating carrots, beetroot and parsnips edged with flat-leaved parsley one year will be followed in the next by blocks of broad beans bisected by arcs of peas edged with dwarf French beans.

This is above all a fruit garden – an extravagant celebration of fruit in all its beauty and for all its flavour. The walls are lined with espaliered plums, nectarines, gages and damsons, with peaches and apricots against the west-facing walls. An avenue of quince trees lends a simple geometry to a long rectangular space known as the Quince Lawn, bounded by yew buttresses used to create niches containing box topiaries of obelisks and elephants. To the south a large fruit cage shelters all kinds of soft berry fruits – raspberries, blackberries, loganberries – surrounded by

ABOVE One of the happy surprises of the walled garden is the lusciously romantic rose garden, lit up by a vivid blue reminiscent of that used by Clough Williams-Ellis at Portmeirion in Wales in the 1930s.
OPPOSITE Roses, foxgloves and thistles create a pink and white scheme in the borders of the Quince Lawn.

Jerusalem artichokes that grow up to 2.5 metres/8 feet tall. In another area gooseberries and pumpkins are grown together (a curious couple) while in four of the potager beds themselves are pear canopies supported on metal frames. Six 'Williams' Bon Chrétien' pears are planted 90 centimetres/3 feet apart round the perimeter of the circle, trained up and over the 2-metre/7-foot structure with their laterals trained right-handed to meet each other's trunks. At their foot is a froth of spring flowers, underplanted with *Alchemilla mollis*.

There are two glasshouses, where year-round salad crops are grown, as well as forced asparagus and rhubarb, chicory and kale. Salad leaves and vegetables peep from terracotta pots on the terraces outside the glasshouses. Then the wonders of the potager suddenly give way to a gridded orchard as the walled garden slopes down to the north, with sweeping *allées* of medlars and pears forming pathways. Wildflower meadows have become increasingly important at Daylesford, as elsewhere, and they surround the walled garden and also invade it. Beyond the walled garden there are more informal orchard plantings of cherries, walnuts and apples. This estate is also ideal for bulb plantings in that its naturally undulating, free-draining Cotswold land varies from open parkland and mown lawn to beech grove and heavily shaded avenue. Around the entrance drive are daffodils in elongated drifts a thousand bulbs strong: *N.* 'February Silver', *N. poeticus*, *N.* 'Thalia', *N. obvallaris* and *N. pseudonarcissus*. The long arching avenue which is the north drive has benefited from tens of thousands of pot-grown corms of *Cyclamen coum* and *C. hederifolium*. Nearer the house, snowdrops, *Galanthus nivalis*, take over: a hundred thousand bulbs were planted in one autumn alone. There are *Iris reticulata* in the orchard in the walled garden, and fritillaries in the spring-fed glades around the lakes.

From the foot of the walled garden, the visitor descends into a darker, wooded zone and along a scented walk, an important linking device between walled garden and house. In 1998 Golby oversaw extensive thinning of Daylesford's woodland – mainly the removal of a thick scrub of holly – and inserted a heady mix of scented shrubs

A carpet of crocuses prefaces the irresistible orangery, where Warren Hastings oversaw the cultivation of mangoes and other exotics (today it is used as a true orangery, for overwintering citrus plants).

ABOVE The strong bones of
this landscape, and the dignity
of the architecture, stand out
in the snow.
OPPOSITE ABOVE The Pool
or Millennium Garden was
created in a difficult triangular
space in 2000, and makes
for an intimate and luxurious
hideaway.
OPPOSITE BELOW Woven
elephants are one of many
light-hearted 'exotic' or
'Indian' references at
Daylesford.

including daphnes, lilacs, philadelphus, phillyrea, myrtle, osmanthus and sarcococca, several of which are fragrant even in midwinter (the daphnes, most notably). Magnolias and viburnums lend colour and lightness of tone, while honeysuckle and clematis have been encouraged to 'go on the rampage', as Golby puts it. Key shrubs include *Viburnum* x *carlcephalum*, *Syringa vulgaris* 'Maud Notcutt', *Clerodendrum bungei* and *Elaeagnus umbellata*. Epimediums and ferns create intrigue lower down, mingling with hostas in drifts, *Galium odoratum* and *Saponaria officinalis*.

The scented walk prepares one for the setting of the house, which is dramatically undulating and backed by woods, with the house itself poised somewhat austerely above it all. The visitor is aware of the presence of fast-running streams and springs, as well as the two large lakes, which adds to the excitingly fluid and unstable feel of the topography. The lakes were created in the 1780s, together with an interconnecting cascade, a woodland stream and a series of falls. The smaller top lake is decorously overhung by a large plane tree, its edges softened by *Primula florindae* and Siberian iris, though its front edge is kept clear to lend definition to views from the house. Water flows from here down though a dell to the lower lake or Great Pond, its south end enclosed by overhanging oaks. The Dell Garden is a spring garden with hellebores, bulbs, osmanthus, magnolias (*M. kobus* and *M.* x *soulangeana*) and a linking planting of *Cornus mas*. These garden passages are handled with a very light touch; there is a sense that the voids built into the garden's structure allow it to commune with the wider countryside. It is as if the garden has been given permission to exhale.

If the house has a certain hauteur, then the orangery, which sits next to it, is its cheeky sidekick. A gorgeous confection, it was designed by John Davenport to complement Samuel Pepys Cockerell's flamboyant classical-meets-India house, which referred to Hastings's status as the first governor-general of India. Hastings was known for his taste for exotic fruits, including lychees and mangoes, but the orangery today more conventionally houses the orange and lemon trees which adorn the swimming pool garden in summer. This compact triangular space with its pavilion has a Regency Gothic feel, in keeping

The South Terrace, which was created in the mid-nineteenth century, features a box parterre construed along 'Indian' lines.

with the orangery, with romantic, even blowsy, plantings of roses and self-seeding *Eryngium giganteum* amid the citrus trees and topiarized *Quercus ilex* and *Ilex crenata* in terracotta pots. In one corner is a delightfully cool little shell grotto.

Up at the house, the Victorian terrace to the south (by Edward Kemp) comprises a simple parterre in box, to an 'Indian' design, with a pair of mature medlars at each end. But the real horticultural riches are to be found inside the house, where there is a strong emphasis on creative displays of produce and flowers, part of a nineteenth-century tradition which is discreetly kept alive here and at certain other English houses (notably those belonging to the Rothschild family). Pots of foxgloves, clipped and trained honeysuckles, standard redcurrants in moss-topped

pale French terracotta pots (for the dining room) and shrubs such as *Viburnum carlesii* are among the delightful surprises to be encountered in the rooms and corridors at Daylesford. Large spiral-trunked bays and 2-metre/7-foot triple-tier living display stands of *Ligustrum delavayanum* (known as 'triffids') are among the highlights. Globes of French lavender, 90 centimetres/3 feet in diameter, are clipped with sheep shears in preparation for display in the house. The dining table is adorned with box balls and cones in silver flower pots, or common thyme grown to look like an inflated pincushion. Topiary herbs also feature in the rooms: clipped rosemary and lavender balls, bushes and dwarf standards. After a week or so inside the house, the clipped evergreens are taken back to the glasshouse yard and attached to a drip irrigation system which revives them.

Daylesford is an interesting and uncompromising mix of exuberant cornucopia – in the walled garden and in the house displays – and grand restraint, in the wider landscape and woodland. It is a distinctive estate, determinedly ploughing its own furrow.

The Lynn Garden, Ascott
Jacques and Peter Wirtz

This new garden is an abstract arrangement of mounded turf forms, pools and stylized groves of trees.

Ascott is the home of Sir Evelyn and Lady de Rothschild, members of that great banking family which once owned five large houses – Waddesdon, Mentmore, Tring, Aston Clinton and Halton – set amid a continuous 16,000-hectare/40,000-acre estate across a swathe of Buckinghamshire. Today, Ascott is the only Rothschild house in the Vale of Aylesbury that is still lived in by direct descendants of the original owners. The collection of paintings, furniture and porcelain in the house is of international museum quality, but amid the opulence the overall ambience remains that of a functioning family residence. That is because, under the terms of the bequest of the estate to the National Trust in 1949, it is still used a family home. It can be visited on certain weekdays in the summer.

In the mid-nineteenth century Ascott was a modest farmhouse used by the Rothschilds as a small and festive 'hunting box', benefiting from uninterrupted views south across gently rolling green countryside. It was tittified into a large, cottage-style residence by Arts and Crafts architect George Devey in the 1880s, and substantially enlarged later, so that it now has the appearance of a substantial half-timbered farmhouse. Numerous specimen trees were planted in the park in the late nineteenth century, and enclosed formal garden areas were created on the land falling away to the southeast. All of this has been carefully maintained and enhanced by successive generations, and today the estate as a whole has the immaculate feel associated with all Rothschild properties.

Most of the garden areas at Ascott are to the south of the house, which offers expanisve views towards Ivinghoe Beacon and Whipsnade Zoo. But the Lynn Garden (named after Lady de Rothschild) is tucked away to the north-west, entered through a gap in the hedge halfway down the long Serpentine Walk of tall beech hedges that extends on a line directly from the front door of the house. It is an enclosed world, about 0.6 hectares/1½ acres in size, of abstract forms, contrasting textures and shades of green designed in 2006 by the Belgian father-and-son team Jacques and Peter Wirtz, and it comes as a great surprise and delight. The Wirtzes made their reputation in international design through their creation of cool, contemplative formal gardens consisting of straight canals and long green hedges. The Lynn Garden is a good example of the most recent phase of their work, which incorporates sinuous curves into the ground plan, on as large a scale as possible.

The scene is dominated by four grassy mounds of varying character, with several smaller satellite mounds dotted around, almost as if each one represents a different individual or personality. The mound immediately in front of the visitor is a simple dome surrounded by a substantial ring of pennisetum grasses and a beech hedge. All the grass in the garden is normally closely mown, though in recent summers it has been allowed to grow, giving a shaggier look. Across to the left is a perfectly circular island surrounded by a moat, with a stand of *Prunus* forming another circle on the island, somewhat reminiscent of Rousseau's famous island tomb at Ermenonville in France. Beyond this, the third mound is a spiral defined by yew hedges, surrounded by perfectly pleached hornbeams. And over to the right is the fourth and final mound, the largest of all, with a circle of *Malus* (crab apples) at its centre and a banked ring of turf enclosing it (in a radical move, this is being replanted as lavender – 'Hidcote' variety – to create a splash of colour).

There are four principal episodes in the garden, including a simple grassy mound surrounded by pennisetum grasses (above and foreground opposite) and a spiral mound with yew hedges encircled by pleached hornbeam (opposite and background above).

ABOVE AND OPPOSITE A third
mound consists of a small
grove of *Prunus* trees on a
slightly raised island encircled
by a perfect canal, reminiscent
of Rousseau's tomb at
Ermenonville.
OVERLEAF The dominant
circular theme of the garden's
structure – here emphasized
by the 'merry-go-round' of
pleached hornbeam, and
the circular canal – adds to
the sense that the visitor has
entered a dream-like space.

Horticulturally speaking, the Lynn Garden is essentially a young arboretum, studded as it is with groups of young trees, notably oaks (scarlet oak, willow oak, evergreen oak), taxodium or swamp cypress (forming a full stop before the large lily pond at the northern boundary) and yellow-woods (*Cladrastis kentukea*). These will grow in time to lend the space a glade-like character.

The visitor to the Lynn Garden drifts through these spaces in a state of contented tranquillity, as if transported to another plane of existence. There are no straight lines, which enhances the sense that one is gliding around the gravel paths and smooth lawns as if propelled by some unseen hand. Even better: on a public day there is a good chance you will be all alone here, since many people miss the garden, secreted as it is off a long (green) corridor, like Alice's portal to Wonderland.

Great Dixter
Christopher Lloyd and Fergus Garrett

The Long Border is the main showcase of the succession planting which is the hallmark of Great Dixter. This border changes in appearance radically every month from April until October – and in each of those months it appears to be 'at its best'. It is an astonishing achievement.

LEFT Dixter's meadows are treasured by Fergus Garrett, as they were by Christopher Lloyd before him.

RIGHT Dixter is really a small estate where the sloping fields, fast-running streams and pockets of woodland provide a foil to the intensity of the gardened spaces near the house.

WHEN CHRISTOPHER LLOYD died on 27 January 2006, the gardening world lost its most respected and iconoclastic plantsman and author. Many at that point wondered what would become of his celebrated garden, Great Dixter in Sussex. Would it be turned into a hotel, like Rosemary Verey's Barnsley House, or be taken on by the National Trust and lose much of its personality, as at Vita Sackville-West's Sissinghurst? Would this once-famous garden be well tended yet lapse into local-authority obscurity, as did E.A.Bowles's Myddelton House in its time, or would it simply be left to wither away, like a number of other once-great twentieth-century gardens?

Until almost the end of his life this last, hard option seemed the obvious route to 'Christo' (as he was always known). He had a horror of those flower gardens where an attempt is made to maintain the place 'in the spirit' of an owner who is long dead. But this most opinionated of gardeners was not above a change of heart and, as he

explained to me at Dixter just a few months before he died, he was by then thinking seriously about how the garden might best be continued after he had gone.

The house at Dixter was built – well, cobbled together – out of several architectural fragments by Christopher's father in collaboration with the great architect Edwin Lutyens. The garden structure of curving yew hedges on sloping ground was barely altered by Christo, leaving him free to experiment with the plants which were his real passion. Nathaniel Lloyd bought the broken-down farmhouse and its outbuildings in 1910; it had been on the market for a decade already, but Lloyd Senior saw potential in it – at the age of forty-four, he had just given up his printing business in order to spend more time on his passion, architectural history. The mellow, half-timbered Dixter, dated to about 1460, was the perfect project.

Lutyens was engaged to help with the renovation of house and garden, and it was he who decided to retain all the

barns, outbuildings and agricultural features in their original positions around the property, which help give the garden its unique personality and sense of permanence. Lutyens also added a new wing to the house. Perhaps the boldest alteration was the addition to it of another whole building: a medieval hall house, due to be demolished nine miles away, was moved timber by timber to Dixter to form a new wing. Today, one would never guess that this is effectively three buildings glued together.

For the garden, Nathaniel Lloyd and Lutyens decided on a simple system of yew-hedged enclosures, and this has been retained in almost exactly the same form ever since. As Christopher said, 'I was lucky enough to inherit an extremely good design by Lutyens and my father. I expect my father would be horrified at a lot of what I have done, but I am very grateful to him.' Most of the garden spaces at Dixter are situated above the house, which is sited near the top of a valley which runs quite steeply down to the river Rother at the garden's perimeter. This creates a feeling that the garden is hugging the house, almost as if to stop itself from tumbling into the valley. Meanwhile, the slope below the house is left relatively unadorned, as meadow grass and orchard. This intimate and then open dynamic works on the visitor in a subtle but extremely effective way.

However, it is the originality and creativity of the planting that people come thousands of miles to see. As Christopher wrote in his classic book *The Well-Tempered Garden* (1970): 'The basis of good gardening must always be a love of plants, and this love, when found, shines out for what it is and communicates with other plant lovers.' This sense of horticultural communication with its audience is perhaps Dixter's defining feature. 'I think it is completely different from any other garden,' he once said. 'It's got its own personal atmosphere, the feel of a family home and the sense one is in a private garden. That is bound to have an effect on its whole ethos.'

In terms of its style, the garden appears relaxed and almost carefree, a look achieved mainly through rampant self-sowing of favourites such as forget-me-nots, as well as Christopher's bold idea of turning the area in front of the house into a wildflower meadow. But this superficial impression is deceptive: Dixter is gardened at a connoisseurial level that is probably unmatched worldwide, the result of a continuous programme of aesthetic appraisal and alteration which was developed by Christopher and head gardener Fergus Garrett, and is now continued by Fergus and his team. Christopher described this principle as 'successional planting', which makes it sound like a functional method, but of course the soul of the garden lies in the choices made about plants. 'High maintenance gardening is most interesting,' Christopher noted. But he was always aware that the garden works on different levels, depending on the knowledge of the visitor: 'It has to have a feeling of relaxation. People might say, "It looks as if it was all done just like that" – but of course it's not true.'

Fergus was Christopher's head gardener and friend for the last fifteen years of his life and is now in overall charge of house and garden. He lives not at Dixter but in Hastings with his wife and two children. It was vital for Fergus that he had Christopher's blessing to continue the experimental spirit of the garden.

'For years Christo said he didn't care what happened to the garden after his death,' Fergus recalls. 'Then one day he said to me, "You are the future of Great Dixter." Later, when he was dying, he said, "I do hope you will stay on." He said the fifteen years he had had with me had been the happiest of his life. I said to him that if Dixter changed in ways I didn't like, I would leave. He said, "That's fine."

'Actually,' Fergus continues, 'the easy thing would have been to leave. But I thought: I haven't finished here. There's so much to do. And if Dixter ever bored me, or changed for the worse, I'd leave tomorrow.'

The garden's originality and verve are partly due to the working method laid down by Christopher. This consisted of a daily perambulation round the garden which lasted about an hour, during which time Christopher and Fergus would make perhaps sixty decisions, small and large. About half of them were to be dealt with immediately, the rest stored up for the right seasonal moment.

'Everything was looked at and carefully considered,' Fergus says. 'We asked: is it worth it? Does it grow well? Does it stand on its own?' That discriminating method is how such exciting Dixter combinations as red tulips against lime-green euphorbia came to be, or the symphony of dots that is forget-me-nots within cotoneaster. Fergus

Springtime at Dixter produces the first of the joyous onslaughts of colour for which the garden is celebrated, from the blues and whites of delicate spring flowers to the kaleidoscopic vibrancy of tulips planted in massy drifts.

says he continues this tradition today, only now it involves the entire garden staff and lasts all day. 'This is not a fluffy cottage garden that just continues smoothly on,' he suggests. 'It's a place where we've always been expressive. I love this fast-track gardening. I love the quirkiness of big plants and big veg (although Christo thought that was gross), the sense of the countryside being let in.'

It is clear that for Fergus it is perfectly natural to continue in this tradition – anything else would seem strange. But he is also allowing his own horticultural voice to ring out, especially in the emphasis on what he calls 'link plants' including thalictrum, forget-me-nots, bronze fennel and *Verbena bonariensis*. 'Christo would never have allowed this,' Fergus says, gesturing across a border interspersed with cow parsley, and later, a corner beset by spreading *Anemone ranunculoides*. 'I'm more self-sown oriented than he was.' Later, we come across an unusual epimedium, carefully tended – 'He hated those!' Fergus exclaims. Hollyhocks

have also been allowed to spread through the grasses in recent years.

So Fergus has continued the approach he developed with Christopher – but with key modifications. The garden already looks quite different from the way it did in Christopher's time, which is how it should be. It has a much shaggier look overall, with cow parsleys (notably *Ammi majus*) and other diaphanous plants allowed to spread and (especially) take up positions at the front of borders, leaning into the paths. Fergus abhors flatness in planting and talks of the importance of 'movement between the plants', of their being 'connected with each other'. The word he uses most when describing the garden is 'flow'; his emphasis is on the rhythmic use of colour, as opposed to Christopher's more narrative approach, where colours would visibly ripple through borders. There is none of the conscious colour-theming of the Great Dixter of the 1980s and 1990s, and any appearance of clumpiness in the way the plants are

arrayed has gone. 'We don't grow plants by themselves,' Fergus says. 'We try to create music with them.' All this is not to imply that the garden is 'better' than it was before; it is just different, which is the Dixter way.

Christopher's signature – and sometimes rather stark – plant combinations are not quite as loud and expressive, and the old 'one-liners' (plant combinations that are so iconoclastic they make you laugh out loud) are also largely gone. Again, this is how it should be, because such moments were expressions of Christopher's personality, and surely it would not be right to try to replicate them. There is no longer any evidence, for example, of combinations such as yellow achillea, red penstemon and purple nepeta block-planted together (the national flag of the People's Republic of Great Dixter?). This is not to say that Fergus has toned down the garden in any sense; it is more that his plant choices are connoisseurial in a slightly different way, relying on close observation to detail and a certain degree of happenstance.

OPPOSITE At Dixter the complexity of the plant combinations – their forms, colours and textures – is always anchored by the topiarized hedge structure and the solid presence of the house.
ABOVE The Lloyd method – continued and developed today – is to bring a great intensity of attention to every detail of every planting. The truth about Dixter is that it always changes: this precise view will never again be exactly reproduced in the garden – such replication would be seen as failure.

ABOVE As summer develops,
the colour palette is
deepened and enriched,
with plants such as flowering
cardoons and variegated
miscanthus grass used as a foil
to strong colours.
OPPOSITE Away from the Long
Border, the experience at
Dixter is of narrow flagged
paths tightly hemmed in by
burgeoning flower borders.

The experimental regime continues unabated – if anything, it is more intense than ever – with promising plants (or, more usually, three or four close relatives or similar varieties) grown for a season in the stock beds to see how well they do and what their characteristics are. Usually at Dixter anything without a longish flowering season is given short shrift, because the astonishing intention at this garden – which is realized with some success – is to have the main long border appearing to visitors as 'at its best' in every month from the beginning of April to the end of October. No other garden in Britain attempts such a thing, let alone achieves it. To make it work, the border has to be treated like a Formula One racing car which needs constant tweaking and development, with Fergus and his pit-stop team always on the look-out for any areas of failure. Every day is a Grand Prix day at Dixter, which aims to be the world's greatest domestic horticultural extravaganza. Essentially, Dixter maintains an Edwardian intensity of gardening, which is possible only because the small number of staff are among the best there is.

What feels like the principal area of the garden can be found on the rising ground to the east (to the left of the house as one approaches). These hedged enclosures contain a glorious jumble of perennial plants and a few defining shrubs, envisaged as a series of continually changing pictures which grow and meld into each other and then fade away. These pictures or episodes are in fact carefully planned, with an emphasis on vivid, uncompromising colour

contrasts. This is most apparent in the exotic garden below the house, where in Christopher's day large-leaved cannas and bananas vied with red *Dahlia* 'Bishop of Llandaff' and purple *Verbena bonariensis* – signature plants still at Dixter, and a look much emulated elsewhere. The long border at Dixter is justly celebrated, but this garden is unusual in that all of its parts are subject to the same close scrutiny.

All decisions were made on the hoof, as Christopher and Fergus made their daily progress through the garden. In the year Christopher died, Fergus recalls, there were some areas of the garden where they felt more tulips were needed, while elsewhere the self-sown aquilegias had become too prominent. These are the kinds of things that most visitors simply would not worry about – the tulips are utterly magnificent – but it is a testament to the level at which this garden is maintained that all these observations are carefully written into notebooks and acted upon in time for the following season. And it makes a difference. Add together the effects of many hundreds of such small adjustments, and one can begin to understand how this garden speaks to its horticulturally savvy visitors in such a profound and delightful way.

The barn garden, with the sunk garden at its centre, to the right of the entrance front, is one of the more formal areas of the garden. Here, one can

OPPOSITE There are moments of delicacy and restraint at Dixter, too, as with this spring planting.
ABOVE The Exotic Garden, famously the site of the old rose garden at Dixter, still stands as a pioneering exemplar of devil-may-care horticultural exuberance, with its large cannas, yuccas, gunneras and other operatic stars.

The entrance front at Dixter has long been used as a place for displaying pots and other arrangements. It's as if the plants themselves are a delegation sent to welcome visitors, which is as it should be, perhaps.

really see the connoisseur's approach at work. On one visit, a carmine camellia in one corner had been allowed to bleed its petals decorously on to the flagstones, while glowing against the red brick of the barn was a delightful grouping of massed tulips in soft pink and purple, offset by the vivid green stems and young leaves of the massive fig trained against the wall. Everywhere there are similarly inspiring plant combinations on view, sometimes parading rarities to delight the plantsman, but often using humble annual flowers not usually seen in 'gentry' gardens. The watchword is always contrast: do the plants work well together, add up to more than the sum of their parts? Contrast is not just a matter of colour, but of texture and shape as well. Indeed, these latter elements are ultimately more important than colour. 'Christopher always said that first plants had to grow well and, second, their shapes had to work together,' Fergus says. 'Colour was always third on the list.'

Added to the idea of contrast is that of balance. Do the plants create a satisfying picture together? Very often Fergus will change a planting not because of a colour problem, but because the scale is somehow wrong. 'When you take the hips of a rose and put them in a vase with the plumes of a cortaderia, it works well,' he says. 'But when we tried it in the garden, the balance was all wrong.' (Flower arranging inside the house was another important mode of expression for Christopher, and the tradition continues at Dixter today, along with the magnificent display of pots which one usually finds in the porch.) The plant combinations which arise from the application of these strictures and doctrines can be seen hundreds of times over at Great Dixter, making many, many thousands of different plant compositions across spring, summer and into autumn.

Such intensity could easily become wearing after a while, of course, and the meadows at Dixter perform a key function, letting the mind relax after the effusions of the more intensely planted areas. Fergus says that the meadows were always closest to Christopher's heart, anyway.

The sense of authenticity that prevails at Great Dixter is partly due to Fergus's insistence on no signage, only modest plant sales, a no-frills car park (with a superb view) and a general emphasis on keeping things as they have been. But it can mainly be attributed to a confidence in his own decision-making. 'I do stop and wonder what Christo would think,' Fergus reflects. 'But if I decide he wouldn't approve, it doesn't stop me. I do it anyway. Because that is how we worked after the first five years. He'd say, "Okay, you prove to me it works." In the last few years he let me try whatever I wanted. He'd sometimes say, "Oh, you'll grow out of it."'

'It doesn't feel like a garden that has settled down into comfortable middle age,' Christopher observed shortly before his death. Indeed not. With all its intensity, colour, rebelliousness and individuality, this is a garden that has been going through a turbulent yet stylish adolescence for the past half-century and more.

Great Dixter's head gardener is now a chief executive and a celebrity in his own right, in great demand for lectures around the world. But one senses he is still deeply immersed in a daily dialogue with a close colleague who also happened to be his employer. 'You know, what I miss most is his fantastic funny character,' he says. 'There was never a dull day. We had such a laugh, though we were also pretty serious. He'd be rude to one person in the garden, then nice to someone else. He was out of control – in the most wonderful way.' It's clear that in a very real way, Fergus and his friend and mentor are still working together. 'Christo is not hovering over my shoulder,' he quietly remarks. 'He is by my side.'

Great Dixter was always a magnet for the horticulturally minded, and, like many with a talent for friendship, Christopher had the ability to make anyone he befriended feel like the most important person in his world. This led to a certain amount of jealousy and over-possessive infighting among the Dixter confraternity immediately after his death. But now there is a new cadre enjoying the Dixter ambience: a true communal atmosphere has been instigated at the garden, with four talented students each year living in the house who learn to garden the Dixter way, alongside Fergus and his three permanent staff. There is a formidable work ethic instilled by Fergus, but also plenty of fun – including projects such as ladder-making conducted in the barns after hours. As Fergus says: 'There was always laughter at the end of the day with Christo, and that same spirit continues. There is always laughter.'

Througham Court
Christine Facer

THE COTSWOLDS GOES COSMIC at Througham (pronounced 'Thruffam') Court, a lovely stone farmhouse set on the edge of an enviably obscure Gloucestershire valley. Here, designer-owner Christine Facer – whose work could best be categorized as of the Charles Jencks School of Cosmic Gardening – has created a garden which is in part a homage to Jencks's original Garden of Cosmic Speculation in Scotland and partly the expression of her own scientific interests. These exist more on the numerical and molecular level than the semi-abstract cosmological plane of Jencks's domain. Dr Facer was previously a leading research scientist specializing in malaria, until a moment of vocational epiphany led her to hand in her notice at the London hospital where she worked and seek out a professional garden-design course. That was in 1999. Very soon afterwards she started to eye the garden at Througham (which had been a weekend house for Dr Facer and her husband for the past few years) as an experimental ground for some ambitious symbolic design ideas.

Dr Facer has no time for conventional or 'polite' gardens, preferring a space that engages with the visitor in active and explicit ways. She is interested in horticulture and plantsmanship, but this always remains subordinate to the symbolic themes of the garden. Some people will no doubt be horrified that Dr Facer has decided to create this kind of garden here, since the C-shaped farmhouse – its central range dating from about 1720, parts of the rest from 1610 – was subject to renovation by the Arts and Crafts architect Norman Jewson in the 1930s. Jewson was celebrated for his work at Owlpen Manor and Cotswold Farm (both also in Gloucestershire), where he created terraced gardens – and he did the same at Througham, on a slightly more modest scale. Dr Facer has respected this layout, made up of cells or outdoor rooms, but utilized

the eminently malleable structure for her own ends. This is actually quite in the spirit of Arts and Crafts, because the garden-room idea always proved ideal for the expression of idiosyncratic ideas; Charles Wade's Snowshill Manor, also in Gloucestershire, is a case in point since it contains a lot of scientific imagery, such as a garden focused on an armillary sphere. In fact the scientific garden has an excellent pedigree in garden history, and can be traced back at least as far as the systematically arranged Renaissance botanic gardens at Pisa and Padua. The sundial is perhaps the best example of a scientific device commonly used in a garden setting, and this was of course a key element of many Arts and Crafts gardens and something of a cult in the first decades

OPPOSITE The Chiral Terrace celebrates left- and right-handedness in nature and has a sixties Op Art feel.
ABOVE Handmade symbolic features such as this gate emphasize the extent to which the garden is a homage to Charles Jencks's Garden of Cosmic Speculation in Scotland.

of the twentieth century. Dr Facer's ideas might best be understood in this context of scientific gardening.

The kind of garden this is is announced at the outset, for people must pass through the 'Anatomy of a Black Swan' gate to gain entry to the garden from the west. With barbed wire cutting across one corner, this piece refers to those rare and unpredictable events, in both nature and culture, that have a major impact: the 'black swans'. This is a new feature at Througham, as is the Chiral Terrace, which

appears above and on one's left as the visitor approaches the front door of the house. The word 'chiral' is from the Greek for hand, and this small platform-like area, with a sixties Op-Art savour, is a paean to left- and right-handedness in nature, since even-numbered molecules are so designated (something which has proven to be of great use in medical research and other areas). The vibrant geometric floor design is made up of distorted rectangles and triangles in red acrylic, polished black granite and white limestone,

while a two-way mirror and DNA sequences written out on the stone walls serve further to disorientate, though there is method to the apparent madness: this feature celebrates the fact that all DNA sequences known are palindromic – 'though no one knows why', Dr Facer adds. It's an Alice in Wonderland moment in a garden full of such mechanistic apparent absurdities, which are really all expressions of wonderment at the diversity and secret order of the universe. It seems rather prosaic to observe that a big old holly shades

The birch trees which run through the meadow at the foot of the garden are spaced according to the Fibonacci Sequence.

ABOVE Tall flags created
by artist Shona Watts
collaborate to make the
meadow into an artistic as
well as scientific statement.
OPPOSITE The Royal Steps
flanked by purple cordylines
are a mock-grandiose
statement which lead the
visitor up and into one of a
number of self-contained
symbolic enclosures.

this terrace and makes it a pleasant place to be, looking south down towards the more conventional delights of the second terrace, with a lawn, lavender, alchemilla, santolina, marjoram and mature yew topiaries, reminding the visitor that this is the Cotswolds.

There is evidence everywhere of Jewson's facility with stonework design. A fine set of circular steps which owes much to Lutyens takes the visitor down to the informal Italian Garden, with four cypresses, and thence into the meadow beyond. Here the eye is drawn by a snaking white painted line and mown path which winds its way through the meadow (six types of native grass) with white birches as staging posts. This is Fibonacci's Walk, since the birches are spaced according to the ratio of the Fibonacci Sequence, where each new number is the sum of the two preceding it (so it runs: 1, 1, 2, 3, 5, 8, 13, 21, etc.). In the distance is a set of coloured banners on poles 6 metres/20 feet high made by Shona Watts, which strike a dramatic and incongruous note at the edge of Holy Brook Valley; while across to the east is the Pico Mound (the result of some earth-moving in the Jencks tradition) and a quincunx of walnut trees. This last has no symbolic purpose, since this is a garden, as Dr Facer says, of meaning and not-meaning.

The central part of the garden, on the sloping ground south of the house, contains the heart of the programme of symbolism, where all is bounded by high, mature evergreen hedges which create the enclosures. These hedges are beech where the visitor first penetrates this inner sanctum, from the western, more naturalistic side of the garden. A corridor runs north–south, with a sculpture of a crouching woman by Rick Kirby at one end. But immediately ahead, laterally across this green corridor, is the astonishing sight of a set of steps with a bright red carpet, lined with spiky purple cordylines. This fanfare of a feature, the Royal Steps no

LEFT The Starburst pool of on-edge slates forms the central point of the cruciform hedge layout.

RIGHT The mysterious Bamboo Grove, formed of 120 black and yellow bamboos in clumps, whispers and sways in the slightest wind.

less, takes one up to a pleached lime walk, where in spring tulips in red, white and black ('White Triumphator', 'Queen of Night' and 'Apeldoorn') mingle with *Allium* × *hollandicum* 'Purple Sensation', replaced later in the season by lavender and white agapanthus. From here there is another surprise, in the form of a dramatic sudden view down to the perfectly striped croquet lawn below, with small yew balls and tall pointed pyramids, reached via the crinkle-crankle Origami Steps of white marble and limestone. This is a little jewelbox of a garden – or perhaps it is a Pandora's Box?

Passing by this garden the visitor emerges at the Starburst pool of blue and purple slates laid alternately on edge around a dark pool (occupied by a large toad, Dr Facer remarks). The pool marks the centre point of a cruciform of four gardens.

The Bamboo Grove to the east consists of 120 black *Phyllostachys nigra* and golden *Phyllostachys aurea*, the darker form on the inside. There are metal plates for stepping stones and a table and chair at the centre. When the wind blows, the whole thing sways, so that it feels as if one is in

ABOVE The Cosmic Evolution
Garden is the highlight of
the contained gardens, and
features 'cosmic' plants such as
yellow *Ligularia* 'The Rocket' in
the Eclipse Shadow Bed.
OPPOSITE Six numbered
limestone spheres honour the
numbers which (we are told)
govern the universe, each
sitting on a mirrored plaque
inscribed with an apposite
quotation.

a boat. It is immensely satisfying looking through the stems of the bamboo; this is a sensual garden, not a dessicated exercise in theory. The Bamboo Garden gives on to the Zigzag Arboretum, where Dr Facer pursues arboricultural interests including *Cercidiphyllum*, *Paulownia*, a fastigiate tulip tree and *Davidia involucrata*. In spring there are masses of tulips as well as hellebores and angelica, while in autumn the maples add new colours. Dr Facer is particularly fond of 'hot' colours from the likes of kniphofia, monarda, knautia, helenium, echinacea and persicaria, preferences on display in the fertile crescent that is the arcing South Border, on the next terrace up towards the house.

The Cosmic Evolution Garden is arguably the heart and highlight of the garden, a castellated yew enclosure dominated by six spheres of Ancaster limestone sitting in puddle-like mirrored ellipses inscribed with slogans such as 'Our Lives Are Numbered'. Each ball represents a planet and is inscribed with one of six numbers which are believed to govern the evolution of the universe, related to phenomena such as clouds, gravity and nuclear energy (this whole feature was inspired by Martin Rees's book, *Just Six Numbers*). The mirrored Black Hole Seat sits at the top of the space, seemingly sucking everything in, while the triangular Eclipse Shadow Bed strikes through the heart of the matter, with black *Ophiopogon* underplanting a collection of plants with cosmic names, such as *Ligularia* 'The Rocket' and *Cosmos bipinnatus* 'Cosmonaut', or those with star-like qualities, such

as the flowers of *Actaea*. In some ways this is a garden of belief, in that scientific theory is being revered and lauded here – but light moments such as this punning flowerbed undercut any potential feeling of scientific hubris.

As one gets closer to the house, things begin to settle down again, though even the kitchen garden has a theoretical spin, since the numerical sequence of Pi is written along the length of the Corten steel which edges all the beds. Again there is an undercutting device, which comes with the knowledge that Dr Facer's West Highland Terrier is named Pi, the steel edging 'running around the garden' just as the dog likes to. The Sunken Garden adjacent to the house is an original Jewson design and has been left in its traditional form, with attractive planting in light and dark tones: Iceberg roses, tulips in black and pink early in the season ('Black Hero' and 'Angélique'), and later dark dahlias such as 'Nuit d'Eté', 'Chat Noir' and 'Arabian Night'.

Dr Facer's garden at Througham Court betrays several acknowledged influences, including, as well as Charles Jencks's cosmic landform gardens, the confrontational poetic adventure that is Ian Hamilton Finlay's Little Sparta. But the designer's particular scientific-aesthetic sensibility ultimately comes through as a highly individualized take on the possibilities of garden-making. After all, we now accept that a garden can be about anything at all – not just plants, or nature in a wider sense – and more and more garden-makers are beginning to exploit the possibilities bound up with that conceptual realization.

The garden begins to normalize (slightly) up near the house, where the Arts and Crafts Sunken Garden designed by Norman Jewson is given a more conventional planting treatment – though the bench reminds one that this is an exercise in cosmic gardening.

Crockmore House
Christopher Bradley-Hole

TRAINED AS AN ARCHITECT, Christopher Bradley-Hole is a thoroughgoing modernist, committed to the doctrines of functionalism, asymmetry and architectural unity that design ideology espouses. Having made his name in the 1990s as a landscape designer creating sleek, minimalist spaces, Bradley-Hole has during the past decade been exploring the possibilities of naturalistic planting and the ways it might intersect with the traditional modernist aesthetic. Like the majority of contemporary British garden designers, he has been influenced by the New Perennials school of planting from the Netherlands and Germany, favouring the use of grasses and sculptural perennials used repetitively across large areas of planting, or else subtly varied in terms of form and variety within a single species.

The turning point for Bradley-Hole – and garden modernism – was a Chelsea Flower Show garden in 1997 which successfully blended the modernist architectural aesthetic with the naturalistic, spaced-out style of the New Perennials look, with a particular emphasis on grasses and irises. This garden came as a relief next to the crammed herbaceous extravaganza which traditional British garden style had become. A typical Bradley-Hole garden design unites formalist rigour with exuberant but carefully planned drift plantings of grasses and perennials such as rudbeckias and echinaceas. At several gardens he has taken this methodology to its logical conclusion in formalist terms by creating a simple (but large) grid of planting squares, designing each one individually yet allowing for rhythms and echoes to develop between them. The result is a burnished, moving ocean of plants awash with golds, blues, purples and reds.

At Crockmore House, in Oxfordshire, Bradley-Hole has utilized the grid-bed system which has become something of a signature for him. From above, the gridded pattern is blurred into indistinctiveness in summer and autumn when the plants have grown up – especially the miscanthus and stipa grasses which form the planting structure – but there is an extremely rigorous underlying aesthetic, with each bed exactly 2 metres/7 feet square. In this case the grid is laid out adjacent to an old orchard, where the contents of each square bed seem to echo or pre-empt the next.

Behind the red-brick, neo-Georgian house the visitor emerges on to a massive terrace area of seasoned oak decking and York stone, picked out in squares and half-squares as it hugs the edges of the building and its conservatory. A series of large terracotta pots filled with grasses enhances the sense of larger than life luxury. The deck's perimeter is cordoned off with tautly stretched wires, through which peep an exuberant range of perennials, from half a dozen varieties of *Miscanthus sinensis* (including 'Morning Light', purple-flowered 'Ferner Osten' and arching 'Flamingo') to *Verbena bonariensis*, *Sanguisorba officinalis* and *S. caucasica*, *Monarda* 'Ruby Glow' and *Knautia macedonica*.

From here the exceptional landscape can be enjoyed: undulating fields rising to a ridge fringed with oaks, with not a house or road in sight. The perimeter of the garden, about 50 metres/160 feet away, is defined by a deer fence, 2 metres/7 feet high, hidden by a planting of miscanthus (including *M. transmorrisonensis* – 'almost an evergreen') punctuated by bursts of the white feathery *Persicaria polymorpha*. To the right one can see the grid beds, while over to the left is open pasture and a circular

From a distance, the 'orchard' plantings at Crockmore House appear to be one seething masses of perennials and grasses – but in fact Christopher Bradley-Hole created a severe grid system of thirty-six squares to provide an underlying structure.

LEFT AND RIGHT The generous decked terrace immediately gives on to an artificial bank which is richly planted with perennials, and thence to a mown circle in the meadowland beyond, providing a visual stepping stone between garden and landscape.

OVERLEAF The gridded nature of the design can be discerned more clearly here. There are repeats across the piece, but each square also has its own internal planting rationale. Over the hedge to the right is the substantial vegetable garden.

mown area which is understood as a continuation of the berm-like rim which was constructed to create the raised front edge of the terrace, and to deal with the significant change of level from house to garden. For Bradley-Hole, the open grass space has something of the stone circle about it. It certainly provides a valuable visual staging post between the intense ornamentalism of the garden and the landscape unfolding itself beyond. The bank curves around two sides of the terrace, with the grasses (the miscanthus, *Pennisetum alopecuriodes* 'Hameln'

and *Deschampsia cespitosa* 'Goldtau') as its foundation, highlighted by splashes of vivid red penstemon 'Firebird' and slightly darker 'Garnet' in the foreground, rivulets of *Sedum* 'Herbstfreude', flashes of *Persicaria amplexicaulis* 'Atrosanguinea' and *Monarda* 'Ruby Glow' singing out. The knautia weaves its way through the scene, while the bronze fennel offsets the greens. Mahogany-flowered *Hemerocallis* 'Mrs Hugh Johnson', *Achillea* 'Terracotta' and creamy-white *A.* 'Mondpagode' provide more structural interest, with their contrasting forms.

Despite the impressive roll call of flowering plants, at no seasonal moment do the bank plantings appear to be complex or overwrought. And they can be enjoyed as much from afar as up close. Bradley-Hole uses a relatively small spectrum of colour in his gardens. He does not like to use yellow because, he says, it can 'break the spell' too easily. He favours what he calls 'moody' colours – dark purples and reds – which resonate over a long distance and create a diffused pictorial quality.

This look is carried through to the grid beds themselves, a series of thirty-six square beds on a grid pattern, like test beds at a horticultural research establishment. But there the similarity ends, because each bed is a careful composition, viewable from four sides, using perhaps a dozen perennials and half as many grasses. There are planting echoes between the beds that help unify the scene, and by late summer, when the grasses have grown up, the paths become invisible from a distance and everything segues into a single image. 'I see the composition as a whole, not as a series of beds,' Bradley-Hole explains.

The rich ornamental planting here utilizes a similar palette to that on the bank, augmented by a range of other perennials including *Agastache rugosa*, pink *Dianthus carthusianorum*, purple *Aster* x *frikartii* 'Mönch', *Lysimachia ephemerum*, the stately white spires of *Veronicastrum virginicum* 'Album' and *Digitalis ferruginea*. A particular favourite is *Thalictrum rochebruneanum*, with its reddish stems and purple-pink flowers. In the beds farthest away from the house, the height increases to about 1.5 metres/5 feet, with *Stipa gigantea*, *Eupatorium purpureum* 'Atropurpureum' and *Angelica gigas*. Beyond the eighteen beds of perennials are two rows of fruit trees set in a formalized wildflower meadow (mainly oxeye daisies). And then a series of raised beds for vegetables, screened off by a beech hedge.

Naturalistic plantings have always looked good up against the smooth white or grey concrete of modernist buildings, or bordering the expansive cedarwood decks familiar from the Californian modernist tradition of

Persicarias of different kinds, fennel, veronicastrum, *Digitalis ferruginea* and *Verbena bonariensis* are among the perennials used in the gridded beds. Bradley-Hole became entranced by the possibilities of this kind of planting at an early stage of the development of New Perennials.

Thomas Church and others, but Bradley-Hole has gone much more deeply into planting philosophy than any of his modernist forebears or contemporaries. The style is really a sophisticated development of the early realization of modernist designers (including Christopher Tunnard and Le Corbusier himself) that a naturalistic planting style suits modern architecture very well indeed: partly because of the simple sense of contrast between smooth and 'shaggy'; and perhaps partly, too, because it expresses something of the idealization of form that is redolent of buildings of this genre.

In classic New Perennials style, in the autumn the big grasses (especially miscanthus) come into their own, offering a palette of burnished bronzes, russets, golds and purple-browns.

Pettifers
Gina Price

TUCKED INTO A FIELDSCAPE of lovely diagonals, the garden at Pettifers is a north-facing but open rectangular space on several descending levels, with exceptionally elegant views towards rising hills in the distance. This friendly, low-slung village-centre house, of caramelized Cotswold stone and dating from the seventeenth century, might appear to herald a conventional Oxfordshire garden for conventionally minded Oxfordshire people. But Gina Price, the genius of the place here, has in recent years cultivated a genuinely innovative attitude towards planting which has had an influence far beyond the boundaries of the county.

However, the garden was not always a radical experimental plot. 'The garden was very old-fashioned before,' Gina recalls, referring to its early 1990s incarnation. 'Lots of *Geranium psilostemon* and three great clumps of *Hebe* 'Boughton Dome' along the front of the border.' Following repeated visits by knowledgeable and opinionated friends, notably the sisters Diany Binny and Betsy Muir of Kiftsgate Court, cottage favourites such as these were all ejected, as were roses en masse, catmint and almost all the silver-leaved plants. These horticultural encounters encouraged Gina to start gardening at a higher level in her 0.6-hectare/1½-acre plot, and in particular to start making truly connoisseurial choices in terms of the plants used. In the years since, through constant application and with the regular help of a talented gardener, Jonathan Wood, formerly of Hidcote, Gina has achieved a great deal.

LEFT The garden at Pettifers is a carefully balanced arrangement of spaces (notably the open lawn), shapes (the decorative urns and topiaries contrasting with more natural forms) and colours.
RIGHT One of the distinguishing features of the garden is the way views back are treated with as much care as the prospect out.

ABOVE At the foot of the lawn is a formal enclosure of topiary, with tulips in spring, massed dahlias later.

OPPOSITE The edges of the garden artfully devolve into areas for bulbs and flowering shrubs and trees (including the pink magnolia).

Talking to Gina, who is admirably keen to give credit to her friends, it soon becomes apparent that what happened next came to her instinctively. She extended this vigorous editing process from the principles of pure plantsmanship into the realm of spatial and structural design. There is a sense in this garden today that everything is there for a reason, in terms both of the planting and of formal features such as walls and hedges. It is rare indeed to come across an English garden in which that is the case, because the tradition has generally been an effusive, cottage-style look in which obvious design is somehow seen as vulgar. There are probably several thousand owner-gardeners in Britain who are today working with plants at the highest level, but there are perhaps only a few hundred who have the ability to use space imaginatively, to create a meaningful sense of progression in the garden and to think of plants for their form and rhythmic role in conjuction with the garden's structure. Invisible gardening, you might call it. For this reason Pettifers is well worth visiting, and perhaps especially so in autumn and winter.

Gina's editing process initially meant more horticultural reduction. 'I just started hating all those lumpy shrubs and I took about twenty out,' she says. As a result the planting structure is now largely dependent on tall grasses such as miscanthus and cortaderia, while a policy of dividing plants has led to deliberate repetitions through the borders. Gina acknowledges the influence of the Piet Oudolf and the New Perennials movement, though, like her friend Graham Gough of Marchants Hardy Plants in East Sussex, she

feels she could not do without colourful prettiness in the English manner. Any New Perennials piety about colour being a peripheral concern is vigorously undercut at Pettifers by gestures such as the use of orange, purple, pink and white dahlias in the yew-hedge enclosure in the lower, far end of the garden, which produce a polka dot effect against dark foliage. 'This way you can get blocks of colour with less maintenance – 150 blooms of a single plant,' Gina states matter-of-factly. But the basic structural change reconfigured the garden, introducing a sense that garden spaces and borders alike have been designed to work together, in a way that is somewhat reminiscent of Phyllis Reiss's Tintinhull in the 1950s or Lanning Roper's perfectly weighted work of the 1970s. In fact this garden brought to mind something Sylvia Crowe said about Tintinhull in her *Garden Design* (1958): 'No plant, however lovely in itself, is grown unless it contributes to the picture, and those whose form and colour are needed

again and again . . . are constantly repeated. In spite of restraint it is anything but austere.'

So in the main east-facing border flanking the lawn at Pettifers we find in spring abundant tulips ('Ballerina', 'Deirdre' and 'Blue Parrot') and alliums (masses of 'Purple Sensation'), followed by kniphofias and daylilies together with more unusual subjects such as the yellow *Ratibida pinnata*, which looks like a cross between a rudbeckia and an echinacea. Always there is the structure of grasses underpinning everything – miscanthus varieties, cortaderia, vast panicums, molinias. In the right-hand border – which was 'very itsy-bitsy before', Gina says – a ribbon of *Aster turbinellus* flows like a river in autumn, replacing a similar effect produced by daylilies earlier in the season, through and around sedums, asters, achilleas, scented-leaved geraniums, euphorbias and photinia. There is an emphasis on simple and strong duality in plant combinations: at the front of this border *Euphorbia*

griffithii 'Fern Cottage' ('the best of the red euphorbias') offsets the *Rudbeckia laciniata* 'Herbstsonne' which grows over it; elsewhere at different times one might find *Miscanthus sinensis* 'Nippon' next to *Aconitum carmichaelii* 'Royal Flush', *Filipendula ulmaria* 'Aurea' growing by 'Ballerina' tulips, or masses of monkshood (a Pettifers favourite) placed with panicum grasses.

'I learned a lot one day from a Dutchman who came here,' Gina reveals. 'He said he was bored with Sissinghurst. Then he looked at some plants in my border and said, "Look at the leaf, they're all the same." Now I always try to create a contrast in leaf form between plants which are next door to each other.' This is emphatically not the kind of glorious 'muddle' proposed by Margery Fish and the proponents of cottage planting.

The underlying structural theme at Pettifers is the long horizontal. This is apparent from the first, in the unusually wide and shallow front garden that spans the

Colour tones are carefully organized, from a relatively narrow base, as with the dusky purples of alliums and bistort above, to areas enlivened by jabs of bright flower colour such as the orange opposite, and objects like the sky-blue bench.

entire frontage of the Prices' honeyed-stone seventeenth-century house. A front garden is not usually a place to linger, of course, but the narrow range of elegant plants here, such as *Buddleja agathosma*, the white *Scilla peruviana* and *Euphorbia characias* 'Joyce's Giant', heralds the consideration and panache to come. At the rear, the visitor enters the garden via a side door from the kitchen and is immediately faced with another long rectangle, in the form of a gravel path inspired by the one at York Gate garden, with criss-cross brick decoration that emphasizes its length. This top garden is an awkward shape bounded by a curving wall and overshadowed by a vast beech tree.

ABOVE Flask-shaped yew topiaries stand sentinel in the intimate landscape of fields and parcels of woodland. Gina Price believes in solid bursts of colour, provided here by vivid agapanthus.

OPPOSITE Grasses are used decisively in this garden.

OVERLEAF Gina Price's confidence with form can be seen here, with kniphofias at the front of the border contrasting with softer surrounding forms, and tall miscanthus grass abutting daisy forms of helianthus, all given structural definition by the topiary and hedging.

It has also been formed into a series of rectangles, with the lawn cut geometrically to lend a feel of order and decorum. The dappled shade here led to a decision to make it into a spring woodland garden, with bergenias, cranesbills and a multitude of different hellebores. Also here are the dark globular forms of *Pittosporum tenuifolium* 'Tom Thumb', acers and evergreens – 'I believe you have to have evergreens near the house, for winter,' Gina maintains. The path quickly turns a right angle and leads down via stone steps through several narrow and shallow (and rectangular) terraces and out on to the rectangular apron of lawn, flanked by the borders which are the main decorative event of the garden. The rectangular theme continues as one descends to the farthest section of the garden, where a formal hedged enclosure with four Arts and Crafts inspired yew pillars seems to span almost the entire width of the space. This is yet another shallow rectangle, a reminder of the front garden at the beginning.

BELOW Here feathery stipa grasses offset the flat-topped forms of achillea varieties and sedums, raised to a higher pitch by the presence of the bench, which the plants do not overwhelm. Randomness is abhorred at Pettifers.

OPPOSITE Among the many excitements to be enjoyed in this garden are combinations of plants which more conventional gardeners might deem to be too close in colour to mingle.

Perhaps it seems a little dry to point up the geometry of the garden: few visitors will leave raving about rectangles rather than Gina's use of plants. But it is this sense of structure above all which helps raise the garden far above the ordinary. 'I look at things with a photographer's eye,' Gina says. 'If you can do that, it's amazing what you can teach yourself.' She is talking about the way a garden photographer will always seek out or create a compositional structure in any view, a premise which has translated into Gina's gardening on the ground.

Pettifers is a garden that is rich without being overstuffed with plants. Its lines are simple, but there is great complexity and interest within those boundaries. Gina now thinks as carefully – perhaps even more carefully – about what she might take out or omit, as about what she might put in or retain. The garden is not particularly large, and is of a conventional rectangular shape, but a sense of movement and progression has been introduced through the careful

exploitation of changes in level (with the drama of the yew enclosure as the garden dips at its far end) and by the use of strong plants which 'announce' different episodes in subtle ways (such as a pair of sprightly *Hakonechloa* grasses in light green glazed Brook Pottery pots on the top terrace path, a contrasting colour tone to the dark and rich colours nearby). The use of walls and hedges is not overdone because they are often so far reduced that they merely imply boundaries and divisions without the need for a major intervention. The garden 'speaks' to its surrounding landscape through the use of complementary shapes – the open lawn mimics the expanse of fields in the vista beyond – and framing or perspective devices, such as the columnar Irish yews asymmetrically placed at the ends of the main borders by the lawn. The garden works as well in reverse as it does on the journey out; the route back opens up all kinds of new vistas and perspectives on things already seen, such as the main borders by the lawn suddenly visible at eye level. All these things appear to have been achieved instinctively at Pettifers.

'Designers go on about features,' Gina says, 'but it's really all about atmosphere. So few gardens have a real feel to them.' Such a feeling can be intrinsic to the place, but it can also be made anew by a gardener or enhanced through close attention to detail throughout. As these pictures show, there is nothing 'mushy' about Gina's planting design – everything is presented as the result of deliberate aesthetic decision-making, with panache and sure-footedness (combined with fleet-of-footedness, seasonally). If one wants to understand the difference between traditional English cottage gardening and gardening of this order, then a visit to Pettifers will provide the best illustration. Happenstance is not quite good enough, here.

Pampas grass (*Cortaderia selloana* 'Pumila') explodes from the borders from summer into early autumn, its plumes striking an exotic note in the Oxfordshire countryside, and contrasting with the columnar Irish yews planted at the end of each border.

Waltham Place
Henk Gerritsen

DUTCH GARDENER and nurseryman Henk Gerritsen was in some ways the philosopher of the 'Dutch Wave' of naturalistic plantsmen in the 1980s and 1990s, the movement which came to be known in Britain as New Perennials. His friend and collaborator, and the putative leader of the movement, Piet Oudolf, has never been particularly comfortable as a writer; Noël Kingsbury, another key figure in New Perennials, has provided a voice for the movement over the years by co-writing texts with Oudolf. But in these illustrated books, which have a practical, how-you-can-do-it-yourself slant, Oudolf has generally restricted himself to practical observations regarding plant choices and combinations, effectively creating an aesthetic botanical taxonomy based principally on observation of plant forms and their habit in the wild. There is little or no theory (doubtless a relief, to many).

Gerritsen, on the other hand – with a degree in history and politics and an earlier career as a painter – always sought to place his own attitudes to horticulture in the context of the wider culture (as did another New Perennials theorist, Rob Leopold). He produced two books with Oudolf, both of them focused exclusively on the palette of plants used in 'naturalistic' New Perennials gardening, describing this horticultural armoury as 'an assortment of strong, easy-to-maintain and versatile plants that stand out by virtue of their robust shape while still looking natural', and adding: 'It's especially thanks to Piet's sensitivity [that he] started searching for plants that were able to enhance and complement the powerful architecture of his designs, and ended up with an assortment of plants that fuses together these extremes: robust, architectural indomitability and playful fragility.'

Gerritsen plundered this palette himself in his own garden and nursery at Priona in the Netherlands, which he developed over some thirty-five years after a visit to

OPPOSITE The plantings in the Square Garden at Waltham Place are at the wilder fringe of the New Perennials school. The white plumes of *Persicaria polymorpha* dominate, contrasting with the 1930s brick pergola that cuts through the centre of the space.
ABOVE The wooden gazebo in one corner of the garden provides a vantage point. The cloud-pruned hedge in the foreground is nicknamed 'the caterpillar'.

Mien Ruys's garden in 1977 which changed the direction of his life – he realized on the spot that a garden can be an artwork. 'About fifty years ago Mien Ruys described her garden philosophy as "a wild planting in a strong design",' he later explained. 'My planting is much wilder and my design much less rigid than hers.'

Gerritsen never shied away from prescriptiveness, however (one of the besetting paradoxes of naturalistic gardening). 'For my own use,' he stated, 'I formulated this rule of thumb: what is straight should be curved, what is curved should be straight. Meaning: in a garden where everything is straight – the walls or hedges around it and the path through it – the secondary landscaping should be curved: sloping or freakish paths, hedges, lawns or borders. And the other way around: in a freakish or shapeless garden, the secondary landscaping should be straight.' But he later conceded: 'Over the years, my ideas about garden design became more structural. Because quite soon it became obvious that my garden needed landscaping. The wilder the planting got, the more the need for a strong design evolved. Wild plants in nature don't grow in a disorderly mish-mash, but grouped three-dimensionally in recognizable plant communities and in harmony with the scenery.' There is a synergy here with Keith Wiley's ideas about planting (see Wildside, page 310).

These ideas were not publicly aired until the end of Gerritsen's life, when in 2008, a few months before his early death, he published his *Essay on Gardening*. Produced by Architectura and Natura of Amsterdam (the imprint of one of the best garden bookshops anywhere), this passionate polemic (a book-length 'essay') must stand as one of the most original and interesting garden books of recent decades. In it Gerritsen set out his philosophy of gardens in typically idiosyncratic, highly personalized and anecdotal fashion. For Gerritsen, 'Gardening is an unnatural pursuit. The gardener views nature as an abundantly filled grab bag from which he is free to select a number of items he would like to use in his garden, and then dispose of the rest in the trash. But he's mistaken: once opened, the grab bag turns out to be Pandora's box, which constantly releases demons that besiege the gardener and his garden.' He saw horticulture as a battle which the gardener was always destined to lose – in fact he felt it was not even worth joining battle with nature in the first place: 'The maintenance of my garden must never degenerate

into a battle against nature. If that happens, or threatens to happen, I'm doing something wrong. Plants that can't live without the use of chemical fertilizers or pesticides don't belong in my garden. Not in any garden.'

Thus Gerritsen developed an intensely relaxed attitude to looseness, randomness, failure and happenstance in gardening. He actively encouraged wild flowers and even weeds as an aspect of horticulture, developing a system where plants were left to fend for themselves, where the death of organisms was as celebrated as their life. He pushed the wild garden aspects of New Perennials to extremes no one else dared or cared to go to. While Oudolf's work can be described as positively decorative in some of its phases, with clever intermingling of plant structures and habits across a wide horticultural canvas, Gerritsen is disposed to let it all hang out, to let his natural 'philosophy' of planting dictate the mood instead of conventional horticultural tinkering. (One could not imagine Gerritsen being let loose on a major public project such as New York's High Line, as Oudolf was.)

Aside from his own garden at Priona, and his final publication, Gerritsen's greatest legacy is the garden he created at Waltham Place in Berkshire for the Oppenheimer family. The garden at Waltham Place is now maintained very much in the Gerritsen spirit (the head gardener is ex-Priona), at the naturalistic extreme of the New Perennials spectrum, with some emphasis on the South African flora which is the birthright of the owners.

Mr and Mrs Oppenheimer inherited Waltham Place (which had been in the family since 1910) in 1984, and were always enthusiastic about English wild flowers, but it was only in 1999 that, during a tour of Dutch gardens and nurseries, they discovered Priona and Gerritsen. Client and designer proved to be a complementary pairing.

The main gardened area at Waltham Place is the half-acre Square Garden, enclosed by seventeenth-century brick walls and stridently bisected by a massively proportioned, rose-bedecked pergola added in the 1930s. Just as at Great Dixter (see page 86), an inherited formal layout proved to be the perfect setting for experimentation with plants. (And in fact Gerritsen, here and elsewhere, was increasingly relying on artificial interventions – principally hedges and topiary – to act as a counterpoint to all the wildness.) Most of the lawned areas were torn up and transformed into deep planting areas, which cannot really be called 'beds'. These

are shaped in amorphous fashion, as is a great cloud-pruned hedge which the designer nicknamed 'the caterpillar'. Here is Gerritsen's straight/curvy dichotomy in action.

A good vantage point for viewing the mass of perennials and grasses jostling for survival here is the turreted corner gazebo. In one area, massive plumes of *Persicaria polymorpha* together with purple thalictrum and veronicastrum tussle with the ground elder which was allowed to remain (the weeding regime is simply to pull out clumps of it now and again).

ABOVE The brick pergola was part of the 1930s redesign of this walled garden. An Italianate pool was added at the same time. Gerritsen was happy to work within this formal framework.
OVERLEAF The tone of the plantings in the Square Garden subtly varies, with one part of the garden dominated by white perscaria mingled with purple veronicastrum and tall grasses, while other areas contain collections of sun-loving specimens and smaller grasses.

LEFT Gerritsen's design philosophy is predicated on the tension between straight lines with formal structures, and curving lines and amorphous forms. The dichotomy is encapsulated in the relationship between the pergola and the 'caterpillar' hedge.

RIGHT The classical formality of the box-hedged compartments in the so-called potager – adjacent to the Square Garden – is undercut by the naturalistic plantings, which tend to be dominated by a handful of species in each season.

A gravelled zone features pink crinum lilies, blue agapanthus, red and yellow phygelius and dieramas. Masses of *Miscanthus* 'Gracillimus' surge behind the box hedge, while cardoons and euphorbias add to the strident, form-driven, outsized theme of the planting (plants that can battle weeds must have a thuggish side). The atmosphere is quite unlike that of any other garden – a completely unbridled and unburdened feeling, it has an ever so slightly dangerous edge to it. This is gardening at its wildest, caught at the moment before it descends into plain messiness. Speaking shortly before his death, on this point Gerritsen was implacable (as he was on most points). 'You can take it further than I do, but those gardens are messy – there's no structure. It isn't nature. Nature is not a mess; it is very orderly and very logical. People don't ask why a plant is growing somewhere – there is always a reason. That's very different to a garden: but what you have to do in a garden is introduce the same

kind of logic – the feeling that it is right, but you don't know why. Plants are not decorative creatures; they are living things with a purpose and a place.'

Attached to the walled garden is the so-called potager, with sections demarcated by low box hedges in traditional manner, though the planting is anything but – a changing menu which tends to be reliant at any given moment on a dominant species, such as poppies or *Erigeron annuus*. This part of the garden feels like a mansion where the parents have gone away and the kids have thrown a wild party.

The wider estate and farm at Waltham Place, including a substantial kitchen garden, is run strictly on organic principles (it is inspected by the Soil Association), with the meadows managed to encourage wildlife. The principal rooms of the house look out and down what might in another garden be a great double border, 85 metres/ 280 feet long. Instead, horseshoe bays of beech hedge have been created, each containing *Stipa arundinacea* grass.

Horseshoes of beech hedge, each with *Stipa arundinacea*, make an unusual substitute for a traditional double herbaceous border leading off from the house and its terrace. The supporting plantings also bear no resemblance to traditional horticulture (Gerritsen always claimed to be bored by pretty borders).

The plantings in the beds along this walk also resist the categorization of 'border' plants, with substantial clumps of verbascum, euphorbia, grasses, self-sown teasels and burdock, against burgeoning buddleia and the bindweed which here is valued for its flowers (and was even at one point encouraged to grow up specially made supports – though it characteristically did not oblige).

Gerritsen acknowledged that his own style intervened with the processes of the wild – 'I'm not imitating nature – there is a personal touch in the work' – but he insisted at the same time that the gardener should be looked upon as part of nature, not simply as someone making an artifical pastiche of it. For him, gardens were a continuation of wild nature, simply organized in a slightly different way. Above all (and this is a theme which crops up time and again in discussions of twenty-first-century planting design), he emphasized the importance of observing plant communities in the wild. 'You can't improve on nature but you can intensify the experience,' he said. 'In a garden you have many more plants than in nature – but I'm inspired by nature, not by other gardens. I hardly ever visit gardens. I'm not interested in all those beautiful borders.'

Highgrove
The Prince of Wales and others

The tree-studded lawns that flank the Thyme Walk leading up to the west front of the house are a sea of daffodils in spring.

THIS GARDEN is in some ways a paradox. The private residence of the Prince of Wales (since 1980) and the Duchess of Cornwall, situated just outside Tetbury in Gloucestershire, Highgrove was for many years one of the most famous gardens in Britain – yet open only to a privileged few. There was a time when people would whisper that they had 'seen Highgrove' – as if it was some kind of Cotswolds Eldorado.

Things have changed in recent years, and now groups and individuals are welcomed on a regular basis, though the house remains private. In 2010, for example, some 38,000 people visited Highgrove, all on prebooked tours with considerable security checks (visitors have to bring passports). Not so much of an Eldorado now, then, but still a much-coveted garden visit. A stylish visitors' entrance, the Orchard Room,

has been built in the guise of an amusingly detailed neo-classicized farmhouse, with pudgy Ionic columns.

The general layout of Highgrove is that of a compact landscape park, its proportions similar to the kinds of nineteenth-century *giardini all'inglese* or *jardins anglais* which can be found in Italy and France. Formal compartments around the house give way to pasture (in this case wildflower meadows, too) dotted with arboretum trees, and a woodland belt to the south. There is a large walled kitchen to the south and there are more formal compartments near the estate buildings and offices to the north. One suspects that Hidcote was the original inspiration for the designed garden, in that the formal, compartmented areas seem at certain moments to be reaching out to grasp the landscape. But the scale is bigger here. The specimen trees in the encircling parkland give Highgrove the character of an arboretum, with some of the trees skirted with low box hedges. Beeches are a speciality: Highgrove has the national collection, complemented by the colourful stems of dogwoods in winter. There is a strong sense of enclosure – not surprising, given the security constraints.

The garden as a whole impresses with a multiplicity of moods and episodes, as well as evidence of the finest craftsmanship throughout, which is just as one would expect, given the Prince's well-known support of traditional rural skills and values. And there is one great set-piece view, which would find its place in the pantheon of memorable moments in English gardens whether or not this was a royal domain. This is the celebrated Thyme Walk, which leads up to the west front of the house, playing the part of a grand entrance drive (the actual front entrance, on the other side of the house, is modest). This carpet of multifarious thymes is flanked by delightful dumpling-like topiaries of golden yew and a pleached hornbeam hedge along its length. It is perfectly in scale and keeping with the rational Georgian fenestration and balustrade of the west front (the latter a happy addition by the Prince's architect), and provides a sense of centrality and focus in a garden that is characterized by its many disparate elements. The Thyme Walk achieves the trick of creating a feeling of privacy and intimacy without shying away from the large scale.

The other specific elements of Highgrove garden which have been widely and justifiably celebrated are the Stumpery and the wildflower meadows. It is these three features that resonate most ringingly and sweetly in visitors' memories.

The main wildflower meadow at Highgrove, to the south of the house, was created some thirty years ago with the help of Dame Miriam Rothschild and, although it took some time to get established (the clay soil was rather too rich), it is now justly celebrated as a pioneer of its type. There are two main phases to its flowering. Indigenous and other bulbous wild flowers appear in spring – mainly wild daffodils, together with fritillaries, camassias and alliums – more recently augmented by four kinds of native orchid: marsh, southern, common spotted and early purple. May to July sees a yellow and purple display of wild flowers growing amid quaking grass, agrostis, sweet vernal grass and meadow foxtail. Yellow rattle is a strong (in every sense) flowering component, complemented by twenty or so other common wild flowers, including yarrow, knapweed, oxeye daisy, viper's bugloss, lady's bedstraw, cowslips, ragged robin, sorrel, betony and red clover. The meadow is maintained as a traditional hay meadow, in that it is cut back in August to 4–7cm/1½–3 inches in height, with the grass being allowed to dry out for a week or so (and turned over if wet) so that the seed can drop back into the soil. The hay is then removed and the area is grazed by Hebridean sheep until October. This suppresses the grass, obviously, but in addition the animals' hooves trample the wildflower seeds into the soil, increasing its chances of germination the next spring.

There is now another, quite distinctive wildflower meadow at Highgrove. This is the excitingly named Transylvanian Meadow, inspired by the Prince's intimacy with that region – he has had a farmhouse in the foothills of the Carpathians since 1988. Raised from 'barn sweepings and more targeted seed collections', this vibrant meadow is characterized by Transylvanian variants on familiar English wild flowers, such as bird's foot trefoil, red clover and yellow rattle. Tuberous pea flowers and meadow clary are among the more elegant components of this interesting experiment, which is one of the first things visitors see at Highgrove, since it is situated in pasture in front of the Orchard Room.

If the Thyme Walk and the wildflower meadows are two of the most impressive features of Highgrove, then the third is the work achieved in collaboration with Julian and Isabel Bannerman in the woodland areas to the south and south-west, of which the Stumpery is only the best-known element. The Bannermans specialize in gardens filled with topiary, romantic plantings, small buildings and ornamental features inspired by the classical garden vocabulary (obelisks, for example, and root houses) which they modernize by the use of a variety of different materials and inscriptions. Green oak is a particular favourite, often used in place of stone. It gives their work a certain Miss Havisham meets William Kent atmosphere.

RIGHT Camassias are abundant in the informal avenue which leads up from the woodland belt and kitchen garden to the south front of the house.
OVERLEAF The Thyme Walk is flanked by a clipped hornbeam stilt hedge and leads up to a statue of a Roman gladiator. Extravagantly clipped, dumpling-like yew topiaries add a light-heartedness which is a leitmotif of the garden.

The Bannermans' sensibility is a good match for the Prince's own preferred style, which is gardening with a sense of humour, devil-may-care panache, historical awareness and not a little emotion. They have the skill and delicacy to work in this milieu without descent into kitsch or whimsy. It is notable that many of the features they have created at Highgrove have a highly personal significance for the Prince, which he is happy to reveal to visitors. That curious royal job description of having to live a life of great privilege under intense public scrutiny leads to an easiness about intimacy with the public which naturally lends itself to expression in garden features (much as it did among garden owners in the eighteenth century).

The Stumpery and the twin kiosks which seem to contemplate it can be found at the heart of the woodland. The Highgrove estate is flat, and wants water, and the woodland as a whole adds a dash of excitement and a sense of movement through space. It is delightful to discover the Stumpery in the midst of it: a lorry load of ancient stumps (many of them sweet chestnuts from Cowdray Park in Sussex) were dumped and then sorted by the Bannermans. They piled them up into a kind of sculpture or *fabrique*, which in time sprouted all kinds of ferns as well as hellebores and euphorbias, giving way to a varied display of hosta leaves (these plants being a particular enthusiasm of the Prince of Wales – he holds a national collection). The two small formal yet rustic kiosks, which in their form resemble the sentry-box garden seats that were popular in the 1730s and 1740s, have had their pediments filled with pieces of bleached driftwood resembling deer antlers (these and deer knuckles being traditional materials in such buildings). When he saw the Stumpery, the Duke of Edinburgh apparently enquired: 'When are you going to set fire to this lot?' That sort of humour is quite in the spirit of the place, of course. Paths of ammonite wind through the ensemble, which at one point forms a stumpery arch reminiscent

RIGHT The rear of one of the 'sentry-box' kiosks in the woodland, with a driftwood-filled portico. The garden is replete with such historically nuanced features.

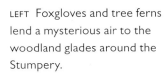

LEFT Foxgloves and tree ferns lend a mysterious air to the woodland glades around the Stumpery.

of grotwork tufa arches found in eighteenth-century landscape gardens (such as Painshill in Surrey, where the Prince is patron).

All these historical references are quite deliberate: even the map of the garden given to visitors is a knowing take on the early eighteenth-century engraved bird's-eye views which are part of the lexicon of British garden history – found in the successive volumes of *Vitruvius Britannicus*, for example. The only uncertain moment is the sculpture interpolated here, a crouching nude called *Goddess of the Woods*, by David Wynne, which is a perfectly good thing in itself but appears out of tune in these surroundings. It's an example of the 'one thing too many' malaise which occasionally bedevils Highgrove.

A more recent addition to the woodland is the *Temple of Worthies*, a memorial to the late Queen Mother, with a bronze portrait medallion of Her Majesty in her gardening hat, against a sunburst. The memorial itself takes the form of a chunky pedestal with rusticated detailing topped by a similarly dimpled stone pyramid. It is a startling and original addition achieved with vigour, a celebration of a life rather than a mournful reminder of death.

As the visitor follows the woodland paths, all kinds of diversions come into view, from hydrangeas in flower (which add to the sense of being in a French landscape park) to whimsical topiaries (a boxwood snail 'eating' a hosta, perhaps), to William Bertram's impressively tall gingerbread-house-style treehouse for Princes William and Harry, and ornaments such as a giant terracotta urn, a gift from Sri Lanka. The woodland is a repository for numerous such ornaments and objects. As the official historian of the garden, Candida Lycett Green, explains: 'The Prince . . . is given an inordinate number of presents.

RIGHT ABOVE The treehouse designed by William Bertram for Princes William and Harry.

RIGHT BELOW The Stumpery is one of the most original features at Highgrove.

OPPOSITE TOP LEFT Julian Bannerman designed the *Wall of Gifts*, incorporating various pieces of masonry given to the Prince of Wales.

OPPOSITE TOP RIGHT Black cranes browse near a tufa (limestone) outcrop topped with gunnera.

OPPOSITE BELOW Highgrove's memorial to the Queen Mother, set within a rusticated base.

The south-eastern end of the woodland belt devolves into a small arboretum of trees chosen for spring and autumn colour. Secreted within are statue groups and Prince Charles's very private retreat, the hermitage-like Sanctuary, made from blocks of Highgrove clay.

These range from whole collections of apple trees or ferns to statues, seats and other garden objects in every variation of style from all over the world. Many of these must be planted or placed for diplomatic reasons alone, giving the garden an eclectic and occasionally eccentric feel.'

It must be akin to having an army of domineering aunts who regularly send odd gifts which must be displayed at all costs. But can it really be the case that it is a diplomatic necessity to integrate so many of these gifts in the Prince's private estate? I found myself imagining how an area of the Highgrove estate could be turned into a 'sculpture garden' for decorative objects or knick-knackery which are surplus to requirements, rather along the lines of one of those graveyards for monumental Stalinist statuary in ex-Soviet states. It would make for an interesting diversion.

In fact there is an area at Highgrove which reflects just this kind of solution. The Bannermans created the *Wall of Gifts* out of odds and ends of carved masonry (many of them

students' offcuts) as well as pieces of more noble lineage, such as a stone lion from Villa d'Este. With a stone bench in the middle of it so that one can rest amidst the chaos if the idea appeals, this collection of angular fragments set against a perfect drystone wall nicely undercuts the immaculate nature of the craftsmanship everywhere else at Highgrove. Not that this feature is undesigned or sloppy: Julian Bannerman expressly wanted it untidy, observing that his initial drawing looked like 'something out of the *Beano*'. The estate craftsman deputed to make it (Fred Ind) had the skill and vision to realize it properly. 'We wanted to make a good job of it but Mr Bannerman wanted it all untidy,' he is recorded as saying.

A large collection of tree ferns adds an exotic note to the east while beyond it the rest of the woodland is taken up by a charming small arboretum of trees chosen particularly for their autumn colour, notably acers and katsuras, with cherries for spring flowers. Hidden away here is the yellow-rendered Sanctuary, the Prince's very private hideaway constructed in 1999 from blocks of Highgrove clay mixed with chopped barley straw. With stained glass windows and a steeply pitched tiled roof, the building has something of the air of a hermitage – again, like the one to be found at Painshill, though perhaps here the spiritual dimension is more authentically felt (proverbially, the hermit employed at Painshill in the eighteenth century had to be 'let go' after being found in the local pub).

There is a great deal more to be enjoyed at Highgrove, from the immaculate walled garden with a delightful moss-covered fountain at its centre, to the large terrace against the west front of the house, to the sequence of gardens (notably the Cottage Garden) which ribbon, via a pergola, through

the north-west section of the estate, adorned with several small garden buildings by architect William Bertram, such as the stone 'pepperpot' pavilions and a dovecote which can be found on the axis of the Thyme Walk, beyond William Pye's ambitious fountain pool. It feels as if there is a new theme around every corner, and of course everything is top-notch. Here the garden at Highgrove is similar, in terms of its ethos and feel, to the Garden of the Four Winds in Quebec, Canada, the late Frank Cabot's cheerfully derivative pastiche, where everything is likewise achieved to the highest standards, and where an owner has been unafraid of pursuing the most esoteric of design interests.

The Prince's taste in architecture, as evinced at the Poundbury estate and elsewhere, is usually characterized as stridently traditional – either vernacular in tone or neoclassical. In his garden-making, however, he exhibits traits associated particularly with a group of designers working in the 1980s who themselves harked back to

The Sundial Garden against the south facade of the house, vibrant with tulips in spring. This is one of the parts of the garden originally designed with the help of Lady Salisbury.

Edwardian Arts and Crafts models and seventeenth-century 'English Renaissance' architecture and garden design.

This group promulgated a fashionable style of gardening based on a concept of the small formal garden or 'period garden' – essentially a miniaturized version of the parterre gardens of the late seventeenth century. The Marchioness of Salisbury at Hatfield House was the first to start working concertedly in this milieu, and Lady Salisbury was also one of the Prince's earliest and most important advisers at Highgrove. Other members of the group were the redoubtable Rosemary Verey, with whom the Prince enjoyed a long friendship, and Sir Roy Strong, who was invited to Highgrove to advise on topiary, seats and other formal elements. The design vocabulary included box balls, pyramids and low hedges arranged in formal parterres, as well as statuary and garden ornament, both antique and reproduction. Sundials were a must, as were white Iceberg roses and *Alchemilla mollis* in quantity. Examples of such gardens can be found in Verey's books *The Englishwoman's Garden* and – its follow-up – *The Englishman's Garden*. It is no coincidence that at Highgrove the garden compartment immediately to the south of the house – the most important one – was conceived at first as a sundial garden, on the advice of Lady Salisbury.

It could be argued that this strand of garden-making was a rural manifestation of postmodernism, bound up as it was with the emergence of the concept of 'heritage' in the 1970s and 1980s. Books such as *The Country Diary of an Edwardian Lady*, films such as *The Draughtsman's Contract* and the fashion designs of Laura Ashley were all manifestations of a knowingly partial and romanticized, 'picturesque' view of Britain's cultural history.

If postmodernism can be described as the appropriation and rescaling of a classical vocabulary, deployed in a knowing and witty manner, then this strand of garden-making could well be characterized in that way. In contrast to modernism, based around the principle of subtraction in design ('less is more'), this style of garden-making at its most richly confected could be said to be based on the principle of addition ('more, please!'). It is certainly vulnerable to the kind of accusations levelled at architectural postmodernism: that it can quickly descend into kitsch, that it glories in artifice above substance, that it is over-commodified (those 1980s gardens were conspicuously expensive to make). But many of these gardens had (in some

cases still have) great merit and charm. They were retreats which went forward into the past: deliciously paradoxical. Some of them, such as Sir Roy Strong's The Laskett (see page 296), can also be described as highly original.

All this is not to suggest that Highgrove is some 1980s throwback. That period was the garden's creative wellspring, the moment it came into being. Since then it has been constantly revised and augmented by skilled and imaginative individuals all interpreting the Prince's vision in their own ways. And of course there are passages and moments in the garden which represent the Prince's own, unmediated vision. This is a 'new English garden' not because it represents the cutting edge of taste but because important new elements are added to it every few months or so.

So, what to make of it all? It must be admitted that the general consensus is that the garden at Highgrove does not quite hang together as a coherent whole. Paradoxically (again), this is probably a result both of the level of care and intensity lavished on each individual part of the garden and the constant process of experimental revision which underlies it. For the Prince this gets to the heart of what a garden can be, as he explains in his introduction to the book about the garden published in 2000: 'A garden is a constantly evolving thing,' he writes, 'and I find that wherever I go in the world a new inspiration will come to me, or as I walk around the garden a further refinement will suggest itself.'

It's an admirably experimental stance, and there are many good ideas at Highgrove – but ultimately there are just too many of them. As a result one comes away with no clear sense of the garden's personality. Everyone involved over the years – and the Prince of Wales is rightly celebrated for his enlightened patronage – has of course tried to make their own contribution the best thing they have ever done. This is a royal demesne, after all. These different voices have been deployed to create an extraordinarily wide variety of themes and styles across the garden's many spaces.

The Prince of Wales is well aware of the need for some kind of unity: 'Throughout the entire process of developing the garden at Highgrove I have striven to create a physical reflection of what I feel at a much deeper level,' he writes. 'Although I wanted each area of the garden to have its own atmosphere, I hoped that, when they were linked together, the different parts might create an integrated experience that would warm the heart, feed the soul and delight the eye.' The challenge is that the kind of unity required of a garden, as opposed to a working estate, is not chiefly based on evidence of a consistent ethos or attitude towards topics such as ecology. At the scale of a garden, it has to be a more basic visual and stylistic consistency. Perhaps this would have been supplied had the Anglo-American garden designer Lanning Roper lived to fulfil his commission by the Prince to design the garden's spaces back in 1980. As it was, there have been various famous names associated with the planning of the garden at Highgrove, and all the advice provided was probably valuable. But in many instances they have politely disagreed with each other as to the wisest course. (This sort of competition among advisers is another obstacle course which royalty must try to negotiate.) The Prince of Wales has been helped successively by the Dowager Marchioness of Salisbury, Dame Miriam Rothschild, Rosemary Verey, Sir Roy

Strong and latterly the Bannermans, as well as various architects who have added structures to the garden. Taken individually all these ideas and influences are rewarding and enjoyable, but it becomes rather a rich mix when administered together, and in quick succession, as is often the case on a garden visit. As it is, visitors on the guided tours have to cope with multiple fleeting impressions which offer no unity of tone. This is actually a rather enjoyable and diverting experience, so it is certainly not a besetting problem. Highgrove garden has a huge amount to offer visitors – occasionally too much – while specific episodes or passages provide a glimpse of the great garden that, with judicious editing, it could yet become.

The slice of the estate which runs east to west across the northern edge of the garden contains a variety of discrete spaces, including the Mediterranean Garden (left) and the Cottage Garden (right), entered by the remarkable Jodhpur Gate.

Living Wall, Athenaeum Hotel
Patrick Blanc

PATRICK BLANC has over the course of the past decade established himself as the leading innovator and technical exponent of a highly irregular yet unfailingly striking branch of horticultural practice. The aesthetic of the vertical garden or living wall is broadly founded on the sheer delight of seeing a garden scene somehow defying gravity and clinging to the side of a building, a sensation that is heightened in dense urban areas. But vertical gardening is a risky proposition, not to be lightly undertaken. Blanc pioneered this technology and has been generous in publishing his 'secrets', but he remains one of the few practitioners able to guarantee (as far as is possible with any planting scheme) the success and longevity of his projects. Only he appears to have truly mastered the technical issues, creating patterned walls of burgeoning foliage that really do resemble gardens.

Blanc's first vertical garden in Britain was created in 2009 for the facade of the Athenaeum Hotel in central London, overlooking Green Park, and it remains in rude health. It can be fairly said that it is now something of a landmark site – though, equally, it's remarkable how many people walk by this vertical jungle without noticing it, such is the maelstrom of competing visual and aural stimulation in the city.

As a child Blanc was fascinated by aquaria and other artificial environments. He created his first vertical garden as a teenager and simply continued experimenting until he was ready to present his techniques to the world. A moment of epiphany came in 1972, when he was nineteen, and visited the rainforest in Thailand for the first time: 'The trees hanging over the waterfalls were full of epiphytes, mostly orchids, ferns, lycopods and hoyas. Another of my great delights was to see how much the rocks in the forest understorey were covered with delicate little plants with their strange silvery and brownish patterns . . . From

At street level on Piccadilly, opposite Green Park in the very centre of London, passers-by are suddenly arrested by the sight of a burgeoning garden rising up vertically before them. This is the living wall on the Athenaeum Hotel, unveiled in 2009.

The living wall covers the height of the building where it turns a corner. The plants are grown in soil-less felt pouches which are attached to an armature held away from the side of the building to allow air to circulate.

then on, I realized that plants could sprout at any height, not merely from the ground.' Employed as a botanist at the Centre National de la Recherche Scientifique (CNRS) at the age of twenty-two, he subsequently spent many years studying subtropical forests.

He began trying to replicate this natural environment by creating a vertical-garden backdrop to his own aquarium, and the techniques he practised there have been gradually honed ever since. His first (indoor) vertical garden installation was in 1986, and gallery installations followed through the 1990s, until the breakthrough of his first large-scale work in the courtyard of the Pershing Hall Hotel in Paris in 2001.

Blanc's central argument is that plants do not need very much soil – or indeed any soil – to grow well, provided they receive carbon dioxide, water, light and enough minerals. One of his 'secrets' is that these minerals can be absorbed by the plant via rainwater dripping down through the plants on the upper levels, reaching all those below. He came to this realization having observed how plants (including epiphytic plants which grow above ground, attached to trees) survive and thrive in a rainforest environment.

Of the botanical background to the new technology, the flamboyant Blanc – with his green-flecked hair and long fingernails – claims: 'Do plants really need soil? No, they don't. The soil is nothing more than a mechanical support. Only water and the many minerals dissolved in it are essential to plants, together with light and carbon dioxide to conduct photosynthesis.

'Wherever water is available all year long, as in tropical forests or in temperate mountain forests, plants can grow on rocks, tree trunks and soil-less slopes. In Malaysia, for instance, out of the 8,000 known species, about 2,500 are growing without any soil. Even in temperate parts of the world, many plants are growing on cliffs, cave entrances, or fallen rocks. On such very steep places grow many berberis, spiraea and cotoneaster species. Their naturally curved branches indicate that they originate from naturally steep biotopes and not from flat areas like the gardens where man usually grows them. Thus, as seen from nature, it is possible for plants to grow on nearly soil-less vertical surfaces, as long as there is no permanent water shortage.'

This last point, however, highlights a practical and ecological shortcoming of living-wall technology: it needs an artificial irrigation system, which rather mitigates against the claim that this approach is founded wholly on natural principles. Vertical gardens can be extremely vulnerable because of this: if a maintenance person turns off the wrong stopcock and goes away for a few days, in a hot environment the entire living wall can quickly become a largely dead wall – I saw this happen at an apartment building in Sydney in 2011. In England (hardly a hot country), the dramatic demise of the country's first living wall, in Paradise Park, north London, where the water being turned off proved just as disastrous as in Australia, gave the whole idea something of a bad name in its early years.

Blanc, however, claims that vertical gardens will have a beneficial effect on the atmosphere of cities. '[It] is an efficient way to clean up the air,' he says. 'In addition to leaves and their well-known air-improving effect, the roots and all the micro-organisms related to them are acting as a wide air-cleaning surface with the highest weight-to-size efficiency. On the felt, polluting particles are taken in from the air and are slowly decomposed and mineralized before ending up as plant fertilizer. The vertical garden is thus an efficient tool for air and water remediation.'

The key structural element to a Blanc vertical garden is the metal frame or armature, which can be hung against a wall or self-standing, but is never placed directly against a building, as air must be allowed to circulate. The armature provides an air layer that acts as an efficient thermic isolation system. A PVC sheet 1 cm thick is riveted to the metal frame, which brings rigidity to the whole structure and makes it waterproof. A rot-proof felt layer, made of polyamide, is stapled on to the PVC. The roots grow on this felt, which mimics the habitat necessary for the mosses which support the roots of many plants on mountainsides and cliffs. Plants are installed on this felt layer as seeds, cuttings or young plants, in 'pockets' fashioned from the felt. The density is about thirty plants per square metre. Artificial irrigation is provided from the top of the wall; tap water must be supplemented with nutrients. A network of pipes controlled by valves dispenses this nutrient solution containing the dissolved minerals needed for plant growth. The felt is soaked by capillary action with this nutrient solution, which flows down the wall by gravity. The roots of the plants take up the nutrients they need, and excess water is collected at the bottom of the wall by a gutter before being re-injected into the network of pipes: the system is effectively a closed circuit.

Technical issues aside, Blanc is adept at creating swirling abstract patterns of plant material across the facades of buildings, either in single rectangular blocks which appear to be painted canvases made up of living botanical 'pigments' in a surprising range of colours, or on facades with fenestration, where the living plantings create a strong sense of unity and also of individuality.

His creation at the Athenaeum Hotel covers the eight-storey facade around the front corner of the building, and descends to the lower-ground-floor level, where it can be seen through the windows of one of the hotel's public rooms. Here tea is served, or cocktails in the evening. 'Grey skies, a cool, foggy atmosphere, mild temperatures – everything is perfect in the heart of London for growing plants from Chile and New Zealand and from the mountains of South Africa, Japan, Korea and Taiwan,' Blanc states. 'So this was an opportunity for me to plant this vertical garden with *Fascicularia*, *Phygelius*, *Pilea* and the superb *Stachyurus salicifolius*, which grows on the marble cliffs of Taiwan. This "cliff-face" is delicately illuminated at night; moonlight by itself can sometimes be too discreet.'

One wonders whether the guests taking tea in the hotel have any idea of the botanical richness of the plantings

In the evening artificial light casts an eerie glow over the wall. The paradox of the living wall is that it is predicated on natural principles – the fact that so many plants naturally live in crevices on walls with little or no soil – but looks like avant-garde design.

that cascade down around them, for the range of plants is impressive, with representatives of unusual genera such as the leafy *Pilea* (six species from Asia), nettle-like *Boehmeria* (sourced from Blanc's own collecting trips to India and Japan) and the Japanese foliage plant *Elatostema* (four species). More familiar species of euphorbias, bromeliads, ficus and ferns do particularly well. In terms of flowers, the neck-craning visitor might spot *Iris japonica*, *Corydalis cheilanthifolia*, *Lonicera pileata* and *Fuchsia hatschbachii*, as well as rivulets of the bright-pink *Dierama* 'Angel's Fishing Rod' and *Impatiens* species.

I well remember my own first visit to the Athenaeum Hotel's vertical garden, at its launch during the Chelsea Flower Show of 2009, when I was very nearly hit by an unusual viburnum, newly planted high up on the wall, which had been dislodged by winds and plummeted down to earth, landing on the pavement just beside me. For some reason I thought this was all my fault and tried to replant the shrub in one of the ground-level planters, much to the amusement of the other guests. I was discovered doing this by Blanc, who was most concerned about damage to the plant (obviously the correct horticultural reaction).

Other high-profile vertical gardens which have helped make Blanc famous include Parisian projects such as that at the Musée du Quai Branly and the Fondation Cartier. Now there are Blanc vertical gardens to be found all over the world, at museums, hotel squares, offices, residential developments and even an underground car park (in Lyon, 2010), with the designer generally juggling at least six international projects at any one time. Blanc never repeats the same planting regimen from one project to the next, and there is a good diversity across his portfolio. He is clearly as botanically and horticulturally excited as he ever was by the potential of a genre he more or less invented and has made and kept as his own.

Patrick Blanc utilizes a wide range of plant material in his living walls, and no two are similar. There are surprising numbers of rarities, including many unusual species which Blanc has collected himself on trips around Asia.

Trentham

Tom Stuart-Smith
Piet Oudolf

W HEN THE PROPERTY DEVELOPER St Modwen held its first press day at the then dilapidated Trentham, having acquired the site in 1996, I was one of only a handful of journalists – and the only non-local – who appeared at the wind-blown marquee on the part-asphalted parterre to hear of plans so ambitious it was difficult to take them seriously – on paper at least.

In the late nineteenth century Trentham was one of England's great houses, the seat of the Granville family, Dukes of Sutherland, the second of whom oversaw the rebuilding of the house, between 1834 and 1847, to elegant Italianate designs by Charles Barry (who later collaborated with Pugin on the Houses of Parliament), with a vast formal garden to match. Trentham boasts perhaps the finest setting of any landscape garden in England: a lake 1.6 kilometres/a mile long modelled by 'Capability' Brown in the late eighteenth century, prefaced by the massive Victorian parterre gardens and surrounded by a 305-hectare/750-acre estate of low, wooded hills. But from the 1870s the estate went into a steep decline, as the family began to eschew Trentham in favour of their other properties. The reason for this is rather unsavoury: according to papers in the Sutherland archive, Trentham became uninhabitable because of the disgusting smell. The river Trent, which flows across the estate, was used essentially as a sewage pipe for the Potteries towns upstream, and the effluent affected not only the 32-hectare/80-acre lake but also the fountains it fed. The Trent had become, according to one contemporary writer, 'a foul slimy sewer, brimful of the impurities of every dirty crowded town that hugs its banks'. What a horrific parody of Barry's dream of Italianate fountains filled with sparkling water. In 1905 the estate was finally abandoned altogether by the 4th Duke and the house left empty and unstaffed. It was offered to the local authorities but when

OPPOSITE Trentham is a romantic garden for many reasons, perhaps most of all for its catastrophic decline and recent renewal. The lower parterre gives on to the huge lake.
ABOVE A grove of paperbark birches adjacent to Piet Oudolf's River of Grass.

they turned it down it was sold to a building company in 1911 and dynamited. All that remains today is the magnificent porte cochère, which gives a sense of the overall scale of this house; the campanile which divided the three-storey 'public' areas from the two-storey family wing; and the orangery. In addition, various urns and statues survived in the gardens themselves (though nearly all were later pilfered), as well as one of four attractive loggias designed by Barry as a visual link between house and garden. These relics now have a defiant as opposed to forlorn air, perhaps because of all the care lavished on the surrounding gardens.

More recently, the estate was acquired in 1979 by an investor who wanted to turn it into an Alton Towers style theme park, only to find that the subsidence caused by mining in the area had made such a scheme untenable. The National Coal Board itself then bought the benighted site and introduced a nine-hole golf course and driving range. It might reasonably have been thought that Trentham was on a never-ending downward spiral.

However, despite initial scepticism at that 1996 launch, the St Modwen company went on to prove that they were serious about their plans. The chairman (a keen gardener, which always helps) and other executives were patently committed to rejuvenating the garden in an imaginative, contemporary and costly manner – a far-sighted approach not always associated with property development companies. Yes, the plan entailed the creation of a large 'retail village' and garden centre at the entrance to the garden, to fund the renovations. And yes, a separate 'Monkey Forest' of 140 Barbary macaques (later realized) was one of the attractions envisaged by a German partner investor in the more distant woodland. But the men in suits at St Modwen were busy putting together a veritable 'dream team' of planting designers – in the form of Piet Oudolf and Tom Stuart-Smith – with Dominic Cole of Land Use Consultants, one of the best and most experienced historic landscape consultants, engaged to deal with the wider landscape. Serious funds were also made available for the ongoing maintenance budget (a hurdle at which so many privately run restorations fall) and today Michael Walker, formerly of Waddesdon and one of Britain's most respected head gardeners, leads a team of nine who ensure that this garden is presented in tip-top condition at every season.

The Victorian parterre at Trentham was one of the most ambitious ever created, at a time of overweening ambition and expansion in almost every sphere. The lower parterre alone covers some 4 hectares/10 acres, which is an astonishing scale for this kind of formal gardening. But the plan for the gardens was never simply to 'restore them to their former glory'. That approach was rather outmoded by the time the project got underway, after the era of the 1980s and 1990s when the National Trust and others were embroiled in an orgy of garden restoration. Tom Stuart-Smith was engaged to work on a way of presenting the gardens in a contemporary manner while staying true to the sense of theatrical grandiloquence which lies at its heart. His response was to enlarge significantly the beds in the lower parterre – the larger of the two – and to replant them with species which might work well amidst the sheer scale of this landscape. As Stuart-Smith remarked before work had even begun, 'I wanted to create a more intimate experience for the visitor. If we replant the garden as it was [with thousands of annuals], people will just yawn and go away. I want to add more detail but retain the overall sweep and grandeur. The setting is just extraordinary.' The style is broadly naturalistic, with plenty of repeats, particularly among the grasses: miscanthus and pennisetum are deployed in meandering 'rivers' across the beds to pay subtle homage to the presence of the rejuvenated river Trent, in which fish are now plentiful again (even salmon).

The lower parterre slopes down towards the lake at its south end. Larger, more moisture-tolerant plants were used in the rich soil here, including *Eupatorium purpureum*, *Veronicastrum virginicum* 'Lavendelturm' and *Thalictrum rochebruneanum* – favourite plants in contemporary naturalistic planting schemes which therefore crop up repeatedly in this book. The planting is surging and vertical in orientation, not meekly horizontal and supplicatory, as carpet bedding is. The healthiness of the plants is testament to the preparation of the soil in the parterre – it was basically entirely replaced. This is big-sweep gardening, in accordance with the setting, but there is plenty of detail to enjoy, too, for those who seek it out – verbascums, echinaceas, cirsium, dahlias, eremurus and alliums mingling with bronze fennel and euphorbia (which must be kept in check). In the higher-up, so-called 'Mediterranean' beds, more drought-resistant plants have been utilized, with sedum, salvia, euphorbia, phlomis,

helenium and rudbeckia making for a lighter-coloured scheme and a more open feel. A massive collection of bearded irises makes a show in springtime. Plants are generally deployed in groups to create drifts, or else repeated within individual beds, so that the visitor does not feel too absorbed by any single area of planting in this vast space. And it is all framed within the vocabulary of formal Victorian gardening: seven large fountain pools, clipped Irish yew cones and obelisks, balustrading, the remaining loggia and numerous restored or replaced urns.

ABOVE The varied colours from grasses and the dead forms of tall perennials in Oudolf's Floral Labyrinth give the lie to the idea that such naturalistic plantings are, by the autumn, symphonies in brown.
OVERLEAF The verticals of fountain plumes and columnar yews recapture the magnificence of Sir Charles Barry's Victorian parterre, brought into the twenty-first century by Tom Stuart-Smith's plantings.

The trick Stuart-Smith has pulled off is to create naturalistic plantings on this scale without their degenerating into chaos; rather, they appear well balanced within their own exuberance. His discipline with repeated plants, coupled with the garden staff's connoisseurial eye with regard to the overall tone and balance, has led to success. At the foot of the lower parterre, by the lake, is the restored bronze copy of Cellini's *Perseus and Medusa* (1545), a perfect dramatic endnote, with the muscled hero holding aloft the head of the gorgon, his sword gripped in his hand. Across the lake at its far, southern end, a statue of the 1st Duke still stands on Monument Hill, surveying a garden which has now been given new life and meaning.

The smaller, upper parterre is a huge and deliberate contrast, in that it has been restored using short-lived, seasonally changing displays of bulbs, annuals, biennials and exotics. The bedding out style was pioneered at Trentham in the mid-nineteenth century – thousands of colourful annual flowers arranged in geometric patterns to create a magnificent picture which could be viewed from the terrace and house windows (some estate owners, such as the Rothschilds at Waddesdon, liked to engineer new planting schemes overnight in order to dazzle and surprise their guests). The 2nd Duke's talented and ambitious head gardener, George Fleming, worked with his deputy, Donald Beaton, in formulating this style, and it was Beaton who was credited later with promoting it more widely, especially as the 'house style' of Britain's public parks. Fleming and the 2nd Duke worked together much as the 6th Duke of Devonshire did with his head gardener, Joseph Paxton, at Chatsworth, growing hundreds of exotic plants and fruits in glasshouses and experimenting with the latest developments in horticulture. This parterre honours that aspect of the estate's history, and provides a suitably festive allure at the most formal end of the garden, which also has the surest physical connection with Trentham's past – in the shape of the orangery.

Piet Oudolf's work at Trentham complements Stuart-Smith's but is quite distinctive. Interested gardeners will

Old Trentham is seen in its full grandeur in the parterre's main axis, which leads up to a fine bronze copy of Cellini's *Perseus and Medusa*. From Monument Hill, across the lake, a statue of the 1st Duke contemplates the restored garden.

find it instructive to compare and contrast the differing styles of the two plantsmen – the massive changes in tone put paid to any sense that 'naturalistic planting' is a generic style. Oudolf has utilized a simpler and bolder range of plants (salvia, echinaceas, phlox, grasses) in the narrow, linear beds 120 metres/400 feet long on either side of the lower parterre, and also planted up the massive rose pergola,

a restored version of Fleming's original, which runs all the way down the eastern side (at 100 metres/330 feet long, it is apparently the largest such structure in the world). But his main contribution is in the area to the east of the parterre, closer to the visitors' entrance. Oudolf's River of Grass is an elegant composition of swirling waves dominated by just two grass varieties, *Molinia caerulea* 'Edith Dudszus'

and *M.c.* 'Heidebraut', augmented by perennials such as *Astrantia major* subsp. *involucrata* 'Margery Fish', *Astilbe chinensis* 'Vision in Pink', *Amsonia tabernaemontana* var. *salicifolia* and *Salvia* × *superba*. It seems to create its own landscape typology and is pleasantly disorientating in terms of scale, like viewing a jungle from the window of an aeroplane. A blind eye is turned to children running

The lower parterre in summer, with Oudolf's flanking plantings in the foreground and Stuart-Smith's beyond.

through this space and hiding in it. The ambitiously titled Floral Labyrinth is a typical Oudolf contribution, with big drifts of perennial flowers and grasses such as miscanthus, persicaria and achillea, given added poise and definition by the presence of mature trees including a cedar of Lebanon.

The Staffordshire Potteries currently has a reputation for being economically depressed, but Trentham, its jewel, is now the best place in Britain to get an idea of cutting-edge plantsmanship, since two of the world's leading protagonists have been given their head to design spaces of imagination and verve. And the retail village environment is actually a perfectly pleasant and attractive place. The car park is a bit of a monster, and it is overlooked by a budget hotel designed in pseudo-Barry Italianate (which is quite funny), but the shops involved have been selected carefully. The retail village is now somewhere many people think of as a destination in its own right, which does not feel wholly inappropriate because during the past century Trentham had come to be considered locally as a 'place for the people'. At various times since the 1920s it has incorporated a lido, a bandstand, a 'ballroom' (where The Beatles and others played) and boating on the lake as part of its country park identity. Trentham is a 'day out', an extravaganza orchestrated to please and impress visitors, now as ever.

OPPOSITE Clusters of choice perennials add variety to the River of Grass.
ABOVE Oudolf's signature plantings, which have more usually been married with modernist buildings, complement the Italianate architecture of the remains of this house remarkably well.

Plaz Metaxu

Alasdair Forbes

'Dragon's Teeth', one of the sculptural interventions at Plaz Metaxu, a remarkable exercise in landscape poetics in a quiet Devon valley.

'A valley is the topos of its own emptiness.'

ALASDAIR FORBES

ONE OF THE MOST significant new gardens to have been made in Britain in recent decades, Plaz Metaxu – the name translates as 'the place that is between' – is the 13-hectare/32-acre garden of Coombe House on the outskirts of the village of Witheridge, in mid Devon. Its owner and creator, Alasdair Forbes, has been quietly developing the garden since 1992, but it is only in the past few years that is has become known beyond the owner's immediate acquaintance.

As the name suggests, the house is situated in the bottom of a small valley. A stream runs its length, passing a man-made lake at the garden's centre. Into this topography Alasdair Forbes has introduced a series of sculptural episodes which are rich in associative – if not precisely symbolic – meaning. This is an unabashedly 'intellectual' garden: one can gain much more from it if an attempt is made to appreciate the philosophy behind its creation. As he puts it: 'A garden is inseparable from its legends. It needs, as well as walking, reading.'

Plaz Metaxu is one of the very few gardens that is worthy of being mentioned in the same breath as the late Ian Hamilton Finlay's Little Sparta in Scotland. There are superficial similarities between the two gardens, in that both are packed with allusions and delicate sculptural interventions, but the method and motivation are quite different. Where Ian Hamilton Finlay was specific to the point of polemical in his exciting use of fiercely

juxtaposed imagery, Alasdair Forbes has been avowedly non-didactic in the creation of his quiet yet searching interlinked spaces. As he observes: 'How often what is called "the soul of a garden" – its tranquil serenity – is frittered away as shadowless repose.' These are contrasting approaches which underpin each garden's strengths.

There is no set route around the garden; in fact, Forbes says, 'Rather than provoke an ever forwards movement, the garden ultimately prefers to focus attention across, between or back.' The shape of the land itself is the key to that movement, because for him the shape of a valley creates a topographical expression of a caesura, or a place that is between.

The spaces around the Georgian farmhouse, at the eastern end of the estate, feel like the natural place to start. Alasdair Forbes has renamed the ensemble of walled kitchen garden and paved courtyards behind the house 'Distress Retort', a place where 'the garden licks its wounds and gathers its courage; where distress and beauty discover their mutual responsibility to each other, and confinement dreams of expanse.' The main courtyard is a refined space somehow redolent of classical Japanese design, with specimen trees and simple sculptures creating various tableaux, while visitors are requested not to step on to the immaculate brushed gravel. The inscribed stones and sculptures do not betoken tranquil meditation, however, but together conspire to make reference to Hermes, messenger of the gods – whose influence can be felt throughout the garden. Mutable and

The 'Hermes' courtyard behind the house. Hermes was the 'magic darkness in the midst of bright sunlight'. The dark mouth of the pot on the right is, says Alasdair Forbes, 'a hermetic oracle' at the centre of the 'Labyrinth of the Broken Heart', laid out in York paving stones.

mobile, Hermes has the ability to move between mortal and immortal realms with ease, a transmutation which visitors to the garden are encouraged to make.

What had been the drive in front of the house has been transformed into a 'votive' lawn for Artemis (goddess of wild places), while through a gate just to the east is a small area of orchard trees, rich meadow grass and pools renamed for Pothos, who personified the side of Eros responsible for incurable nostalgic longing. These still, immanent, suspenseful, carefully gardened spaces set the dreamlike tone for the main axis of the garden in the valley bottom, referred to in its entirety as 'Lyric Motive'.

The garden stretches westwards along the valley bottom, passing several enclosures of hornbeam and beech hedge named for places in antiquity. Alasdair Forbes talks of a 'fluent, "choreographed" spatial rhythm'. First there is 'Ithaka', and then 'Imbros', dignified by megaliths – before it divides around the long lake which spreads west–east, the southern side elaborating into a warren of shrubberies and copses culminating in the labyrinthine 'Hades' and 'Eleusis' enclosures, the latter named after the site where the goddess Demeter supposedly revealed the secret of eternal life, here placed adjacent to the glades surrounding the focal terminus of 'Hades'. The 'Hades' enclosure, one of many intense pockets of meaning in the garden, is lined with upright slates (simply old roof slates) which resemble headstones.

OPPOSITE ABOVE The front lawn of the Georgian farmhouse, with a stream running across it, has been recharacterized as 'Artemis', a lawn dedicated to the goddess.

OPPOSITE BELOW The garden is filled with enclosures, many of them referring to places in Greek mythology. Here, the stone circle of the 'Nine Muses' heralds the entrance to the 'Ithaka' enclosure.

ABOVE The 'Imbros' enclosure contains two megaliths representing 'Man and Boy'. The megaliths and the surrounding slates are from Delabole quarry in Cornwall.

LEFT The entrance to 'Hades'.
Two lead pedestals beneath
welcoming pineapples are
inscribed 'O einer', 'O keiner',
'O niemand', 'O du:' ('O one',
'O none', 'O no one', 'O you:'),
a quotation from the poet
Paul Celan.

RIGHT The top entrance
to the 'Eleusis' enclosure.
The 'Avenue of the Hours'
can be seen on the hillside
opposite. The lake is
glimpsed to the right.

OVERLEAF A view south across
the lake in the heart of the
garden towards 'Eos' (left)
and 'Eleusis' (centre right).
'Hades' is hidden behind
planting on the extreme
right. In the foreground is a
representation of 'Psyche'.
In Greek, *psyche* means both
soul and butterfly (the latter
here, in marble white).

The stream continues along the northern edge of the lake before tumbling over a cascade and flowing on into fields grazed by sheep at the garden's western extremity, an area named 'Hesperos' (for the evening or western star). Alasdair Forbes describes the use of agricultural surroundings as an aspect of the 'choreography of the fields which I have tried to syncopate'. These outer areas of the garden, on the slopes and on the top of the valley edge, form the garden's 'Pastoral Loop'. From here one can look down into and across the entire garden. The shapes of the enclosures near the lake take on a new significance, and the balance of wood, water and grass in the valley bottom can be appreciated (its elemental simplicity brings to mind Studley Royal, in North Yorkshire, one of Forbes's favourite gardens).

Perhaps the most striking interpolation in this outer part of the garden is the white figure incised into the turf on the southern valley slope which represents Pan and also makes reference to musical notation. If there is a presiding presence at Plaz Metaxu, beyond its living owner/creator, it may be Pan, the figure in myth who is caught most fatefully between the physical and spirit worlds – between nature and the imagination – truly a mediating presence in a garden which celebrates all things that lie between as a nexus of literal and transcendent human experience.

But despite the meaningful episodes it contains, this garden cannot accurately be described as 'symbolic'. Forbes argues that conventional symbolic images are merely 'protocols which rather insulate us against than reveal the true depths of the psyche', and as such they are not part of his method. So although we may know from the map that certain areas are named after particular deities or (more often) places associated with them, they are not adorned with figurative images of Greek or Roman gods, as eighteenth-century gardens tended to be. As Forbes remarks, 'The great landscape gardens of the eighteenth century masterfully matched the Latin to the local.'

But he is at pains to imbue the episodes he creates with a sense of open-endedness, as a way both to give life to the stories which arise in the visitor's mind, and to offer respect and what he would describe as a sense of gratitude to the myths themselves. Plaz Metaxu beckons to the visitor both when one is on the spot and in the act of remembering it.

Alasdair Forbes's supposition is that the mythic figures – or what he describes as 'the level of reality' they represent – are instrumental in reconstituting the spatial character of the different areas of the garden and the individual epiphanies which occur in them. For the creator of this garden, the god is the way the space behaves; the space behaves as it does *for the god*.

Forbes explains: 'The garden, at its most attentive, is the forum for this kind of radical exchange between literal and natural orders of experience on the one hand and metaphorical and epiphanic ones on the other. The "empty" space at the heart of the valley, which ramifies into the garden's numerous other "caesural" spaces, also propitiates this ideal of *transmissibility* between alternative worlds – a cross-over between habitual and "orphic" spatiality – that seems to be the garden's founding open-ended principle. The garden has no wish to coerce the visitor into this kind of double vision, but makes itself as available as it can to such attentiveness if and when the visitor feels called to summon it. Perhaps the immediate pleasure of being in the garden entitles us to come and go between moments of single and double vision, while our remembered pleasure of the garden is likely to be haunted especially by the moments of double vision it gave rise to.'

Forbes refers to a wide range of literature, music and art when talking about his garden. Among his key 'alliances' are the psychologist James Hillman, novelist Franz Kafka and the poets Rainer Maria Rilke, Georg Trakl, Emily Dickinson and Friedrich Hölderlin.

It was the 'archetypal psychology' of James Hillman specifically which opened up the possibilities of this non-symbolic method, proposing what he calls 'a theatre of polytheistic forces' expressive of human vulnerabilities and aspirations. His work at Plaz Metaxu has been to extend them into the realm of spatial experience. 'Archetypal psychology recognizes that the soul needs a vital relationship with the gods,' Hillman wrote, following the ancient Thales' observation that 'all things are full of gods.' Forbes approvingly quotes this passage from Hillman's *Re-Visioning Psychology*: 'If in our disintegration we cannot put our bits into one monotheistic ego psychology, or cannot delude ourselves with the progressive futurism or the natural primitivism that once worked so well, and if we need a complexity to match our sophistication, then we return to Greece.'

In his essay on Pan (that seminal deity for Plaz Metaxu), Hillman suggests that when the god is dead, the stones and water and trees became dead things, too. 'There is no access

OPPOSITE The 'Atlantic Bow' carved into the field of 'Themis', facing across 'Hesperos' to 'Pan', carved in the distant hillside.
ABOVE A detail of the 60-metre/200-foot figure of 'Pan' cut into the steep north-facing slope.

to the mind of nature without connection to the natural mind of the nymph. But when nymph has become witch and nature a dead objective field, then we have a natural science without a natural mind.' He continues: 'When we make magic of nature, believe in natural health cures and become nebulously sentimental about pollution and conservation, attach ourselves to special trees, nooks and scenes, listen for meanings in the wind and turn to oracles for comfort – then the nymph is doing her thing.' The analogy with gardening is clear.

Alasdair Forbes has expanded on the importance of Pan to the garden in an unpublished text entitled 'In Parasitu: The Permission to be Between', and I quote from this here:

Pan, as the pastoral premise in man, is, like Hermes, Eros and Orpheus, a god who produces, not shrinks, betweenness.

Pan is the conscience of uncivilizing values, whom Athens nonetheless revered, and Socrates loved.

Perhaps it was less excusable then, in an agrarian economy, to give way to the mirage (in the profile of realities) of a mono-polis-tic truth.

The reports of Pan's death are always premature.

It is not just misguided, but dangerous and sinister, to suppose there can ever be a 'final solution' to the pastoral premise in man.

OPPOSITE The 'Pilcrow' (new paragraph) sign on the 'Pastoral Loop' between 'Eos' and 'Pan'. Moments such as this interrupt the quotidian pastoral.

ABOVE According to Alasdair Forbes, this sign at the foot of the 'Zigzag' path in 'Eos' promises 'to exalt the valley'.

LEFT An apple-wood phallus for Dionysos.
ABOVE 'Et in Arcadia Caesura' disc, with references to Hölderlin and Heraclitus.
BELOW LEFT A stone inspired by the poet Lorca: the inscription reads: 'The day is not yet a wounded boy.'
BELOW RIGHT The 'Panopticon' ensemble is one of the varied sculpted incidents found throughout the garden.

ABOVE 'Let be be' plaque in the glade of 'Alsos'. A matching plaque further down the aisle of the grove reads 'Finale of seem'. Together they form a single line from Wallace Stevens's poem 'The Emperor of Ice Cream': 'Let be be finale of seem'. The play between 'be' and 'seem' goes through myriad conjugations in the garden.

RIGHT A sculptural group entitled 'Orexis'.

BELOW LEFT Another Stevens reference in the 'Alsos' glade: the 'Final Soliloquy of the Interior Paramour' disc.

BELOW RIGHT The 'Leave Taking' stone at Plaz Metaxu.

It is possible to imagine 'down-to-earth' people damning this garden, and this way of thinking about gardens, as pretentious – but that is one thing Plaz Metaxu is not. The garden is not 'pretending' to be other than it is; there is a deeply felt internally consistent rationale to its structure. As Alasdair Forbes has intimated:

My concern is with the garden as an act of psychological faith, the venture of poetic courage.

The myriad other more practical and environmental concerns of a garden, that always accompany, and sometimes overwhelm me, I keep aside for the description of the garden's growth and history.

Perhaps it is misguiding to make this sharp division.

Yet too little is made of a garden's inner consciences, its poetic recourse.

Too little is addressed of spatial integrity.

In a garden, more often than it is comfortable to admit, in the spaces that conform and enrol us, it is better to be taking off our shoes in our hearts.

If the complexities and inherent challenges of Plaz Metaxu are potentially offputting to those who insist that a garden should primarily be a nice place for a walk and a chat, or a medium for growing plants, then Plaz Metaxu could indeed be enjoyed as a stroll around a Devon valley. But that would be less than half the story. Even for those who enter into the spirit of the garden, the full story of the mysterious garden of Plaz Metaxu will likely remain tantalizingly out of reach. For this is a place that is between.

LEFT 'Ananke': human and divine scripts interpreting the drop of the ha-ha. In granite above, 'Homo Salax' ('Man who is fond of leaping'); in marble below, 'Spuma Fui' (Aphrodite: 'I was foam myself').

RIGHT The 'Trakl' stone (named for Austrian poet Georg Trakl), with one of the two 'Zen Ben' mounds behind. Alasdair Forbes: 'The stone marks the folding or running down of the axis of the garden's "Lyric Motive" before the final cascade is reached.'

Cottesbrooke Hall

James Alexander-Sinclair
Arne Maynard

ABOVE The Terrace Borders at Cottesbrooke terminate in a brick wall and doorway with an eighteenth-century urn beyond.
OPPOSITE The view back from the urn, with Arne Maynard's still oval pool in the foreground.
OVERLEAF James Alexander-Sinclair's Terrace Borders work as an immersive experience, from burgeoning alchemilla and catmint lower down, to foxtail lilies and sprays of valerian above. A weeping beech embraces the farther reaches of the border.

COTTESBROOKE HALL in Northamptonshire is a garden which has been developed with discernment over the past century and more by successive owners, most recently the Macdonald-Buchanan family. Several big names in the world of garden design worked there in the twentieth century, including Geoffrey Jellicoe and Sylvia Crowe, while in the past decade the talents of James Alexander-Sinclair and Arne Maynard have been deployed. The result could have been a cacophony of different voices: however, the cellular nature of the Arts and Crafts structure laid out by Scottish designer Robert Weir Schulz in the 1930s means that each design intervention exists in its own enclosed world. The latest elements – and especially Alexander-Sinclair's long double border, which is the garden's showstopper – are very much in tune with contemporary movements in garden design.

The double border, known as the Terrace Borders, stretches some 60 metres/200 feet from the sunken Monkey Pool Garden on the west side of the house, to a door in the brick wall at the far end, with a romantic eighteenth-century urn just in view beyond. Alexander-Sinclair revamped these borders between 2004 and 2006, of course leaving the strong structure of Irish yew buttresses but removing the yuccas which formerly lent a strong structural feel.

Alexander-Sinclair's plan at Cottesbrooke was for borders which ebb and flow apparently according to their own whims, with no discernible colour scheme (previously this was rather a red border), where the links and repeats bounce backwards and forwards but do not necessarily run the length of the border, or appear at regular intervals. The look he wanted was one of apparently effortless artfulness, with ribbons of perennials and bulb plantings segueing from one into the other, relying on the structure of the yew and the long straight paved central path itself to create a sense of underlying calm and order.

ABOVE The fine red-brick Queen Anne house, the cedar of Lebanon and the buttresses of Irish yew all provide a stable background for romantic plantings.

LEFT Unusually, the double border gives directly on to the parkland surrounding the house, with short flights of steps cut into the bank. This creates a strong sense of release.

(This along with the perfectly proportioned red-brick Queen Anne house of 1702 which presides over it all.) The result is immersive as opposed to pictorial, in that these borders work best at close range, not really making sense when viewed in large episodic chunks, as in the Arts and Crafts tradition of Gertrude Jekyll which held sway in English gardens until the mid-1990s. The overwhelming impression is of being smothered (enjoyably) by a wave of verdant greenery which varies but does not develop along the border's length, interrupting itself with bright periods of colour from dahlias and the likes of *Cirsium heterophyllum* and *Sanguisorba officinalis* 'Arnhem'. The long view down this border is inviting, therefore, but perhaps not particularly engaging, horticulturally, since there are so many repeats. The point is, we are in this border, and involved in it – no longer mere observers in an outdoor picture gallery. It's a garden style that is very much in tune with today: immersive, not pictorial.

White corncockles are the key link plant through the border, an innovation by Cottesbrooke's talented head gardener, Phylip Statner (formerly of Daylesford). *Molinia caerulea* subsp. *arundinacea* 'Windspiel' also wanders through classic herbaceous plantings such as catmint and alchemilla, given extra 'oomph' by foliage subjects including *Melianthus major*, cardoons, echinops and euphorbias, as well as the odd yew ball. In spring the purple sprays of *Allium hollandicum* 'Purple Sensation' make their presence felt – less operatic, perhaps, than the mass tulip display which was originally attempted, only to be thwarted by an outbreak of the disease tulip fire. Later in the season the colour palette deepens, with salvias and especially dahlias stealing the show, led by the deep garnet 'Chat Noir', purple-red 'Rip City' and purple-pink 'Thomas Edison'.

One unusual characteristic of the Terrace Borders is the way they are semi-open on the northern, parkland side, with two flagged paths cutting across them and through the yew buttresses, down steps, through doorways in the brick walls and into other parts of the cellular garden. The intensity of the border is reduced somewhat by these piercings, as if a window has been opened in a scent-filled boudoir – a pleasing and idiosyncratic sensation, this sense that open parkland is but a heartbeat away. The cedars of Lebanon add to the feeling that the borders are somehow separated from but still very much part of the wider estate. This was a spatial trick that Weir Schulz, a rather overlooked designer, excelled at, having the confidence and experience to create geometric plans which nevertheless had some looseness to them. One subtle effect created by this clever imbalance is that the light levels on each side of the border can be radically at variance with each other, so that exactly the same plant might exhibit quite different colour qualities and growing habits, from one side to the other.

Leaving the Terrace Borders at their western end, one enters a zone which has largely been redesigned by Arne Maynard in the last couple of years. An oval pool surrounded by gravel announces a stronger sense of formality and decorum, in line with the distinguished statuary which peoples this part of the garden. Alexander-Sinclair's 'rose garden' – in reality a short *allée* terminating in a blue bench, also dubbed 'The Philosopher's Garden' after a stone gargoyle set above the doorway – is a surprise immediately to the visitor's right on passing through the doorway, with 'Penelope' roses interplanted with alchemilla, bronze fennel, phlox and monarda. Orange 'Ballerina' tulips and alliums arise to philosophize in the spring.

From here it is possible to investigate the wild garden, farther to the west: a delightful ravine garden with a meandering stream and an Oriental willow pattern savour, thanks to the small pavilions and collections of acers which light it up in autumn. Another distinctive feature is a pleached lime avenue terminating in the classical statue of a gladiator, one of several classical pieces distributed across the park, notably a fine Calydonian boar near the entrance front of the house.

Maynard's principal contributions at Cottesbrooke are the Lime Walk Border, a wide walk extending south from the oval pool and hugging the brick wall, and the Statue Walk, which it soon meets, parallel to the front edge of the forecourt to the house. (He has also designed the swimming pool garden and adjacent mount, which is not open to the public.) Across both borders the colour scheme runs from delicate pinks to deep reds and purples, with astrantias (*A. major* 'Claret', *A.m.* 'Abbey Road' and *A.m.* 'Ruby Star') and salvias (*S. lavandulifolia*, *S. nemorosa* 'Amethyst', *S. n.* 'Senior' and *S.* × *sylvestris* 'Dear Anja') playing key roles. Phloxes – including *P. paniculata* 'Anne', *P. p.* 'Cool of the Evening', *P. p.* 'Franz Schubert' and *P.* × *ardensii* 'Hesperis' – add delicacy, while heleniums and monardas create little sunbursts at intervals.

The Statue Walk is so named because it contains four fine statues of classical heroes designed by Scheemakers in the early eighteenth century and originally housed in the Temple of Ancient Virtue at Stowe (where replicas now reside). These treasures are lined up and set back into niches in the yew hedge, and Maynard has responded to their presence and scale with plantings of formally trained roses (William Shakespeare 2000) in metal frames – almost used as topiary – and also repeat plantings of the large burgundy-leaved shrub *Cercis canadensis* 'Forest Pansy'.

Visitors can continue from here to the south front of the house and its magnificent forecourt, which Geoffrey Jellicoe redesigned in 1937 in a modern style inflected by the French Baroque, with massive yew hedges and topiaries, lead statues and white Iceberg roses. But closer to hand is the door into the Pool Garden, the largest of the enclosures in the Arts and Crafts layout, which was originally a rose garden but was simplified and modernized by Sylvia Crowe in the 1950s. It consists of a simple circular pool with an exceptionally generous flagged surround, and deep shrub

LEFT The rose garden is a short walkway lined with 'Penelope' roses underplanted with alchemilla. RIGHT A copy of the classical statue of the Calydonian boar comes into view at the top of one of the flights of steps leading up from the Terrace Borders.

borders set against the mellow brick walls. Some of the roses and magnolias have been retained, but otherwise this garden is currently a blank canvas awaiting the next phase of development in an admirably restless garden.

One edge of the Pool Garden is marked by Weir Schulz's delightfully stumpy pergola, which performs a quick dog-leg turn to enclose the so-called Pine Court, a small square area centred on a pine tree which has now rather outgrown the space. From here the visitor goes through yet another door – always a pleasant sensation in a garden – and into another enclosure of four symmetrical beds centred on a sundial, known as the Dutch Garden (as many more formal enclosed gardens were known in the 1920s and 1930s). The planting designer Angela ('Angel') Collins has created a deliciously ethereal confection of herbaceous perennials and annuals (cornflowers, echiums, dahlias) in place of what was a slightly buttoned-up box-hedged space.

All of these gardened spaces must of course be experienced and understood in the context of the estate as a whole, since the house is surrounded by a park designed with some style by an unknown hand in the eighteenth century. The trees are well looked after and there has been much replanting in recent years. The red-brick house is one of the gems of English architectural history. Taken in the round, Cottesbrooke is a quietly stylish package.

The Pool Garden was redesigned by Sylvia Crowe in the 1950s. Robert Weir Schulz's diminutive but charming pergola creates intrigue in one corner.

Olympic Park
James Hitchmough
Nigel Dunnett

I T ALL BEGAN in the late 1990s with innocent-sounding articles by James Hitchmough and Nigel Dunnett – often in collaboration with their colleagues at Sheffield University – with titles such as 'New Public Planting: Research to Find Some Alternatives to Shrubs for Public Planting Schemes' (1997) or 'The Ecology of Exotic Herbaceous Perennials Grown in Managed Native Grassy Vegetation in Urban Landscapes' (1999). What this research was playing into was the development of a planting philosophy based on the replication of plant communities seen in wild places around the world, which could then be parachuted into public spaces in Sheffield, Bristol, London and elsewhere. The climax was the creation by the Sheffield School (as I dubbed them in 2009) of the meadow and other massed plantings in London's Olympic Park in 2012, scenes which were widely enjoyed and commented upon even by those with no interest in horticulture. Fatuous themes imposed by politicians and bureaucrats on the Olympic Park plan – along the lines of 'A Celebration of the Great British Garden' – were successfully obliterated by the sheer hedonistic pleasure of walking the length of the linear park as it unfolded itself in various aesthetic incarnations and in diverse habitats along the banks of the newly culverted river Lea.

The wildflower meadows in the Olympic Park covered a great deal of the acreage of the park in what were often quite narrow, banked strips, lending them a distinctive appearance, since we are used to seeing wide expanses of meadow planting. They were predominantly gold-themed, thanks to the liberal planting of coreopsis, marigolds and rudbeckia, which can flower in the horticulturally difficult month of August, when the Olympics occurred. Two years' worth of trial plantings on site – involving methods which persuaded these plants to flower later than usual – were dress rehearsals before the real thing. The pinks

of echinaceas and eupatorium also stood out, frequently arrayed in simple but powerful combination with the blues of cornflowers and salvias. These plantings have been described in the past tense because they were always conceived as temporary interventions conceived for the Olympics period alone – they will not be in evidence in the park's post-Olympics incarnation as the Queen Elizabeth Park. But Hitchmough and Dunnett are hoping that the example of their work here might lead to similar schemes being adopted in other British parks, most of which remain in thrall to the garish if festive allure of the Victorian carpet bedding tradition.

The Sheffield School designers were engaged to create the Olympic Park meadow plantings for the 2012 London Olympics – which was quite a challenge, because the games occurred in August. However, by careful selection and some manipulation of flowering times they achieved a range of vibrant plantings with simple contrasts, such as yellow coreopsis and orange California poppies with blue cornflowers.

So what is the Sheffield School all about? This team of academics – backed up by a small army of postgraduate student collaborators on the upper floors of the Sheffield tower where their department is based – is promoting a mode of planting which is even more naturalistic than any of the incarnations of New Perennials, the school of planting design led by Dutchman Piet Oudolf which came to the fore in the late 1990s. New Perennials remains heretical enough for many gardeners in Britain, in that a central tenet is that plants are selected not for their colour qualities, either as specimens or in combination with others, but solely for their form. That effectively throws out of the window a century and more of British herbaceous-border development, which has mainly been about colour-theming in the pictorial 'herbaceous' (in reality mixed) border. The Sheffield School goes even further by suggesting that plants should be selected neither for form nor colour, but solely on the basis of their ecological suitability. Theirs is a scientific, evidence-based approach that has little in common with some of the more romanticized fringes of the organic and native-planting movements (the latter always blighted by its fascistic antecedents, in any case).

Another area where the Sheffield School departs from the approach promulgated by Oudolf, the late Henk Gerritsen, et al., is in the way they seek to allow plantings to create their own internal dynamism – to design themselves, essentially. They are not thinking in terms of drifts of plants working together through the seasons, or of bold combinations of tried and tested ornamental grasses and perennials. What they do is seed prepared, weed-free areas in accordance with scientifically worked out matrices derived from looking at specific plant communities in the wild, from Chile to South Africa to Australia to the Steppes. They light the blue touchpaper, as it were, and then stand back, only intervening in later seasons if it appears things are going badly wrong (when a single species appears to be taking over, for example). The aim is to create gardens which look as if they have arisen quite naturally, without human intervention. 'Enhanced nature' is what they call it. Hitchmough's travels have taken him to South Africa (the Cape), the Russian steppes and the Chilean semi-deserts, and he has used aspects of all these habitats in his work, for the idea is not simply to copy an existing habitat but to be inspired by it and then create something that is practical and appropriate to the British climate.

So, the Sheffield School promotes naturalistic planting design for public spaces that is based on the concept of replicating 'plant communities' from different parts of the world which can thrive in our climate. It involves the formulation of seed mixes which reflect this natural distribution, then broadcasting them across the desired acreage in carefully regulated batches using a grid pattern. The result is intended to reflect the seemingly random and disordered state of plant life as it appears in the wild, though, as Hitchmough points out, in every case this appearance is intimately connected with the particularities of site, soil and climate, and is not in the least bit random. This is design, or rather a methodology or system – which is how he would prefer to describe it – that 'borrows some of the forms of spatial organization' from nature, uninflected by the mind of the designer (or should we say botanical technician?).

In a lecture to the British Society of Garden Designers in 2012, Hitchmough stated: 'Plant events such as flowering are now defined more by time than space.' This is essentially an original and revealing way of describing a planting style in non-visual terms. He is saying that plantsmen such as himself do not think spatially at all, beyond defining the boundaries of their site, leaving the plants to get on with it once they are established. The 'action' in any single planting scheme is not created by the careful juxtaposition of swathes of colours to create rhythm and implied narrative – what Hitchmough rather slightingly refers to as 'traditional block planting' – but is all about the successive flowering of stand-out species in a given habitat. Flowering is just another event in the life of the plant community, something which Hitchmough believes should not be engineered to appear more decorative.

Hitchmough's speciality is planting meadows and prairies in open, sunny situations – his work can be seen at the Royal Horticultural Society's show garden at Wisley, in Surrey, where he has made a penstemon meadow, and at RHS Harlow Carr in Yorkshire, where he created a moist meadow filled with Candelabra primroses. He advised on the plantings at the Eden Project and also collaborates regularly with Tom Stuart-Smith on private commissions, for example at Heveningham Hall in Suffolk, where he has

Kniphofias and agapanthus create a show so startling it effectively upstages Anish Kapoor's *Orbit* sculpture.

been developing a North American prairie landscape since 2004. The feeling in these spaces is romantic and pastoral, as one walks through waist-high flowering grasses, wild flowers and other perennials, but becomes dramatic as high summer approaches and the flowers start to bloom in profusion. Hitchmough 'tweaks' nature to produce the look. 'All we've done is rejigged the composition so there aren't too many different plants,' he explains, 'because the visual impact is much more dramatic if you have twenty rather than sixty species.'

Hitchmough's closest colleague at Sheffield is Nigel Dunnett, a botanist who worked as a garden designer until he was thirty and therefore brings his own particular aesthetic to the mix. His main area of interest is in the planting of colourful swathes of annual flowers – what he calls 'pictorial meadows'. He talks about going to create a meadow with everything he needs (handfuls of seeds) stuffed in his pockets. He is also acknowledged as an authority on

green-roof technology. He has recently been devising 'rain gardens' which reuse rainwater, and has reproduced several such gardens at the Chelsea Flower Show.

Hitchmough and Dunnett are passionately committed to the idea that naturalistic plant communities are good not just for the environment, but for our well-being, too. They say that their urban meadows have been particularly well received and cared for in deprived areas, where rather bald or bleak areas of common land have been transformed by their plantings. Their work has mainly been in parks and town-centre areas, since they rely on public funding for their research – large-scale examples can be found in Newcastle, Telford, Bristol and, of course, Sheffield.

The key text related to Hitchmough and Dunnett's work is their co-edited *The Dynamic Landscape* (2004), in which they stress the social dimension, the realities of maintenance levels in the public sector and the ecological aspect of their proposals. 'Ecological processes include factors such as

regeneration, competition, death and decay, and nutrient recycling,' they write. 'In traditionally cultivated vegetation, irrespective of origin, spatial arrangement and husbandry, we grossly inhibit these processes . . . That ecological worth may be more tied up in notions of process rather than a product is an unsettling idea, as it undermines the foundations of many of our values, which are grounded in commodities, a perspective in time and the current boundaries of the nation state.' The Sheffield School is not apolitical in its stance.

Operating at the more artistic end of the spectrum is Noël Kingsbury, a plantsman who has been strongly identified with the New Perennials movement in planting design over the past decade or so. 'I'm sceptical about the whole idea of designing with plants,' Kingsbury says, somewhat heretically. 'You can do that up to a point – but then natural processes take over. My aim is a much denser, more diverse vegetation than you would normally find in a garden.

OPPOSITE AND ABOVE The meadows were planted in great banks and sinuous beds along the edge of the river Lea – the general feel of the landscape design (by American George Hargreaves) was linear. The meadow plantings were rapidly episodic, and helped create a sense of excitement in the park's outer reaches. Rudbeckia in various forms was a consistent theme.

OVERLEAF Some banks were larger in scale, but the plant range was kept relatively small, creating the sense that the visitor was looking at a self-enclosed space, and that there might be something just as exciting around the next twist in the river or under the next bridge underpass.

There was formal contrast, too, with pink echinaceas set against the rounded heads of eryngiums (below), or the bright ball-like flowers of blue cornflower set amid frothy *Ammi majus* (opposite).

Weeds can be kept down because the plants self-seed and spread.' Kingsbury uses his own garden in Herefordshire as a plot for exploring these ideas, and has recently completed a number of plantings in this style in the centre of Bristol. He generally undertakes one major private commission each year.

The Sheffield School has its critics. Any new form of 'design-less design' might justifiably set alarm bells ringing among professional garden designers – it does sound a little like a negation of human artistic intervention in gardens and landscape, seguing all control to nature in this way. The basic social message of the Sheffield School, that it is a good idea to put a meadow in the middle of a city, is seen by conceptualists and other urban-based designers as inappropriate in most contemporary contexts. Philosophically, they say,

why can't we face up to the fact that most people live in cities, not the countryside? Practically speaking, where can kids play football, if there is no grass left? And in terms of aesthetics, have we just given up on design, subscribing instead to that lame old cliché: 'nature is the best designer'? The Sheffield School approach, this argument runs, amounts to an admission of the failure of planning and of the design disciplines – in fact, the failure of humanity to create suitable urban environments at all.

But the success of the Olympic Park means that the Sheffield School's star remains in the ascendant. We are likely to see more 'plant communities' cropping up in public spaces – and perhaps not just in Britain – in the coming years. One of the benefits of the academic milieu is that those students who have worked on Sheffield School projects (quite a high proportion of whom are from China) will go out and practise a version of this methodology in cities across the world. It used to be that Sheffield steel cutlery was known and valued worldwide; today the city is exporting a horticultural theory which might be described as equally cutting edge.

Here purple origanum, and the dead seed heads of alliums which flowered months before the park opened to the public in August, provide a subtle complement to the landscape design, its paths and furniture.

Temple Guiting

Jinny Blom

Pleached hornbeams emphasize the lateral lines of the principal garden area, which has a predominantly green, white and silver planting scheme enlivened by soft colours provided by the likes of *Iris* 'Jane Phillips' and the silvery edge of cardoon leaves.

THE WORD 'intimacy' gets bandied around a lot in garden writing, and the garden at Temple Guiting in Gloucestershire, designed by Jinny Blom, can certainly be described as intimate in character. But this begs the question as to what 'intimacy' might actually mean in context, since this is actually rather a large garden, with some setpiece moments.

The work of some designers makes the visitor feel as if they are thrilled spectators at a performance – Tom Stuart-Smith's design fall into this category on the whole,

BELOW One end of the canal leads up to the mellow walls of a sixteenth-century dovecot attached to the house. Topiarized forms lend definition to the space at each end.
RIGHT Looking south, down through a line of yew topiaries on the upper orchard terrace, across the long water and into the intimate valley in which the house and garden are so closely pocketed.

as does that of Julian and Isobel Bannerman. But the signature of other professionals – including Blom's and Dan Pearson's, for example – somehow creates a one-to-one feel, regardless of the acreage being worked. It seems that certain designers naturally think and work on a more personal emotional register.

Temple Guiting is a compact manor house, of fourteenth-century origins, built of caramel Cotswold stone, ensconced in a remote corner of north Gloucestershire, an area where small, muddy-bottomed green valleys, grazed by sheep, are enclosed by thickening woodland. Perhaps this sequestered character is what first attracted the Knights Templars to the spot – no trace of them now, of course, save for the village name. The snaking river Windrush passes close by, and there are no long views; the place feels pocketed in the landscape. Blom has accordingly designed a garden of successive pockets, which engage the attention in a highly personal way. The overall experience of a first visit to the

garden is akin to having a slightly too intimate conversation with someone you have only just met; you leave with the feeling that something has passed between you.

Soon after they bought the property Jane and Steven Collins drafted in Blom in 2002 to create a structure for the garden spaces. The principal garden area is a series of three terraces on the west side of the house, focused on a late-sixteenth-century dovecot. The main terrace is a blowsy and glamorous space, defined by a canal 30 metres/100 feet long (and ironically named the Long Water) that terminates in a little pavilion of Regency Gothic character, guarded by four charming, saucer-like clipped yew cushions. The canal is flanked by long lines of fresh-green pleached hornbeam, skirted by effervescent borders of white flowers – agapanthus, foxgloves, dianthus – offset by pretty pinks and mauves that range from dusky to sherbetine, provided mainly by masses of *Iris* 'Jane Phillips', with phlox, campanulas, alliums, peonies ('Duchesse de

Nemours') and the rose Winchester Cathedral. *Viola cornuta* is used in both white and blue forms, while spiky cardoons add some power. The effect is intensely romantic yet highly controlled. The predominantly green and white colour scheme would be dull without the pinks and mauves used as supporting cast. This is a refreshingly clean colour palette that has become something of a touchstone for Blom. The tone is somewhat reminiscent of the work produced by Norah Lindsay at a succession of country houses in the 1920s and 1930s – very light of touch, with none of the earnestness perhaps associated with the recent New Perennials style.

The upper terrace is styled the Upper Orchard, with a double row of apple trees, espaliers and various clematis climbing the walls (*C. armandii*, *C.* 'Huldine', *C. uncinata*). The whole terrace area, with its open, south-facing aspect, was formerly used as a walled kitchen garden and the name is a neat reference to that history. The lower terrace has been divided into five bijou compartments or rooms.

OPPOSITE The rose garden is the farthest compartment from the house. Here, pink roses such as Gertrude Jekyll intermingle with pink astrantias and the structure is underpinned by box balls.

ABOVE Looking east from the rose garden compartment across the other four enclosed gardens which occupy the bastion overlooking the valley.

LEFT One of the compartments is a box garden of low hedges and short spires – a sweet interlude which creates variety, given the floral effervescence elsewhere in this garden.

At the far east end is a potentially over-stuffed rose garden, then a topiary garden with the owners' initials picked out in yew, a garden of box ramparts, a dinky little herb garden, and finally a rose-filled dining terrace by the house in the area previously taken up by the privy. These compact little gardens are subdivided by low box hedging, and are good fun though a little cramped in feel – perhaps not the best structural decision made in the garden.

The overall strong west–east axis is given further definition by the Granary Walk, a new pathway created by Blom along the route of an ancient road (possibly Roman), which extends the width of the garden, above the upper orchard and on towards the guest cottages which have been created out of farm buildings. Narrow and pulsing with the presence of the clipped yew pillars which line it like pedestals in a long gallery, this is an unusual garden feature that works extremely well. The planting is as romantic as ever, but slightly more cottagey in feel, with

classic combinations of alliums, eryngiums, verbascums, asters, *Sedum* 'Matrona', *Alchemilla mollis*, white valerian and *Campanula persicifolia*. Roses are an important element here as almost everywhere in this garden – 'Penelope', 'Prosperity' and 'Souvenir de la Malmaison'.

The Granary Walk extends itself and opens out as it reaches the barn and then the cow byre – now holiday lets with their own gardens. The planting invades the widening gravel path itself here, with agapanthus, fennel and *Iris* 'Dusky Challenger' – unlikely bedfellows with a selection of currant bushes. To the south of the Granary Walk, at the far west end of the main walled garden, is the Peacock Garden, an enclosed, roughly rectangular space with a wonderfully wonky old barn taking up the western end – used as a loggia in a way fashionable in the early twentieth century, but regrettably little seen today. As the name implies, the planting here is much richer and deeper in tone – aquilegias including 'Ruby Port', *Knautia*

macedonica, *Cirsium rivulare*, *Potentilla* 'Monarch's Velvet', *Thalictrum* 'Thundercloud', *Salvia* 'Purple Rain', united by repeat plantings of the bronzy grass *Calamagrostis* × *acutiflora* 'Karl Foerster' and tall foxtail lilies (*Eremurus*). After the purity of the plantings around the canal, entering this space feels like moving from a Degas scene of ballet dancers delicately practising at the barre into a gym filled with bronzed bodybuilders pumping iron.

This is a garden with a sense of fun, and the plantings in the tennis court to the north of the Granary Walk raise a smile: various box topiary shapes form a crowd of spectators – alien life-forms who have somehow managed to get centre court seats at Wimbledon. The walls behind are clad in even more climbing roses and clematis, notably the vari-coloured rose 'Desprez à Fleur Jaune'.

Jinny Blom was a therapist in a previous existence. Today, she produces rich yet refined gardens which make you feel good.

OPPOSITE AND ABOVE The Peacock Garden can be found just off the Granary Walk, and the planting has a different feel. Rich colours provided by the likes of *Cirsium rivulare* and *Knautia macedonica* are further dramatized by the spikes of foxtail lilies (*Eremurus*) and repeat plantings of grass *Calamagrostis* × *acutiflora* 'Karl Foerster'. OVERLEAF Yew pillars pace the Granary Walk, the double border which runs the width of the garden along the route of an ancient track. The planting is predominantly blue and purple, with campanulas, aconitum and frothy white valerian.

Angel Field
BCA Landscape

WORKING IN the conceptualist mode, BCA Landscape of Liverpool is one of the most exciting design companies in Britain today. The company – and more particularly partner Andy Thomson – creates work which seeks to transcend the rationalistic pieties of modernist landscape design that have come to characterize so many city centres – uniform benches, predictable lines of trees, regulation pavers and standard-issue steel litter bins.

In the past decade conceptualism – pioneered by the American designer Martha Schwartz – has established itself as an exciting new force in design. There are now perhaps 250 companies worldwide who are working principally in this mode, as well as numerous shows and festivals that showcase it (even Hampton Court Flower Show, organized by the conservative Royal Horticultural Society, now has its own conceptualist-garden category). Like other conceptualist landscape companies, BCA aims to turn up the volume on experience by introducing bright colour, bold lighting, interesting materials (including plastics), witty comments on the history and culture of the place, and sometimes surreal or allusive imagery. The idea is to tell a story through the landscape, or to make specific reference to its past or potential future through a 'readable' design.

Conceptualism also stands as a correction or counter-weight to the multitude of platitudes voiced and postures adopted about ecology and conservation which are flying around the design world at the moment, as we battle with the conundrum of our apparently deteriorating planet and humanity's collective guilt over it. Conceptualist designers suggest that simply creating simulacra of nature in our urban centres is not the most honest way of engaging with spaces and their users, and in any case has little effect on the ecology of the planet. How much better to create places

Angel Field, at Liverpool Hope University's campus, comprises three main episodes: first, the Orchard (at the top end of the space); then the Theatre Garden, with pool; and finally the angel itself (above) in its own enclosure at the end of the pathway.

LEFT The Orchard is a contemplative grove with seating and carved inscriptions.

RIGHT The Origins Garden within the Orchard consists of a low bubbling pool surrounded by an encircling bench.

which actually 'speak' to people and come to have meaning for them?

Which brings us to Angel Field, a new public landscape commissioned by Liverpool Hope University. The garden, situated amid boarded-up Georgian terraces and desolate streets, is a true piece of *rus in urbe* and it is perhaps telling that it has been neither vandalized nor denuded of its ornaments.

The plan consists of three irregularly shaped spaces which create a link between an existing Victorian campus building and a brand-new concert hall and teaching building. The eponymous angel, a figurative piece by Lucy Glendinning made of resin – which local scallywags apparently thought must be ice – is poised atop a tall column forming the centrepiece of the smallest of the three spaces. It marks the climax of the narrative, and is also a reference to the fact that the farm which once occupied this site was actually called, rather surprisingly, Angel Field.

As Thomson explains: 'The journey through Angel Field begins with a reflective pool set within a copse of native trees – a symbolic wilderness representing the origins of life. Next, an apple orchard set amongst a wildflower meadow produces fruit and nectar to nourish the body. Topiary forms and yew hedges define a performance space where flowers put on a colourful show in beds formed by interlocking Fibonacci spirals; this is the garden of the mind.'

The main entrance to the garden, guarded by a modernist porter's lodge in red sandstone, takes the visitor into what is intended to be the opening section of Angel Field, entitled the Orchard. This consists of a pair of wide rectangular planting beds filled with native wild flowers (bird's foot trefoil, red clover, cranesbills, cornflowers, saxifrage) sheltered by rowan and birch trees, as well as apple trees. Underlying order and rationality are expressed by the fact that the tree canopy across both sections is kept at a uniform height.

In one corner of this first space is the Origins Garden, where a low, bubbling, 'primal' pool is encircled by a stone bench etched with a quotation from Thomas Aquinas: 'Nihil est in intellectu quod non prius in sensu,' 'Nothing is in the intellect that was not first in the senses.' Quotations etched in stone, in the manner of Ian Hamilton Finlay, are a recurring theme in a garden replete with telling details. There are lines from T.S.Eliot ('Where is the knowledge we have lost in information') and Shakespeare, but perhaps most successfully the entire text of 'Pied Beauty', Gerard Manley Hopkins's best-loved poem, which begins, 'Glory be to God for dappled things.' Fragments of the poem in a lively variety of fonts can be found scattered on the ground throughout the Orchard. The design team from BCA (Andy Thomson and Becky Sobell) says these are intended to resemble archaeological remains.

The connection with Hopkins is that from 1879 to 1881 he was a curate at St Francis Xavier Church, whose granite form looms across one corner of Angel Field. His experience of Liverpool was not an entirely positive one, despite the fact he was working in an Irish Catholic church which regularly drew a 7,000-strong congregation and boasted nine priests. The young poet was appalled by the 'deepest poverty and misery' of the city, calling it a 'hell-hole' and concluding, 'Liverpool is of all places the most museless.'

The second section of the design, and its heart, is the Theatre Garden, which was inspired by the rational expression of 'order out of chaos' to be found in Italian Renaissance gardens, pre-eminently Villa Lante. Cutting across the middle of the space is a rill with fountain jets and a line of pleached lime trees. Creamy limestone paving, embedded with etched and coloured tiles inspired by the work of A.W.N. Pugin, forms an informal circular stage by the rill. The audience, or picnickers, can arrange themselves on a smooth green lawn edged by six pom-pom clipped pines. Between the row of limes and the rill is a series of box-edged beds with seasonal displays of perennials in purples and soft reds (*Verbena bonariensis*, *Centranthus ruber* and asters in late summer) organized according to the

Angel Field is replete with carved inscriptions in the manner of Ian Hamilton Finlay's Little Sparta, with quotations from Shakespeare, Thomas Aquinas and Gerard Manley Hopkins (who was a curate at the adjacent church).

Fibonacci Sequence. It's a rich mix, symbolically – perhaps rather too rich – but on the ground it works.

Thomson points out that this project was always conceived as a garden, as opposed to a square or courtyard, so was intertwined with horticulture from the start. With reference to the implied journey through the garden, from the body to the mind, he describes it as a 'contemporary Renaissance garden'.

In traversing Angel Field the visitor moves from the origins of time and space (the Aquinas pool), through disordered nature and wilderness (the Orchard), into manmade rationalism (the Theatre Garden) and finally to the heavens, accompanied by the angel. As a garden design it's an ambitious undertaking which is largely successful. It is the story of an evolution which has nothing to do with Darwin.

OPPOSITE AND ABOVE In the Theatre Garden echinaceas, asters and other bright flowers fill box-edged beds arranged according to the Fibonacci Sequence. Cloud-pruned trees enhance the contemplative feel of the space.
OVERLEAF A bubbling rill is another component in the layered linearity of this unusual design.

Hanham Court
Julian and Isabel Bannerman

JULIAN AND ISABEL BANNERMAN have one of the most distinctive voices in British twenty-first-century garden design, and the garden they made at their home, Hanham Court in Gloucestershire, was until recently something of a touchstone of their singular style (they moved out in 2011, after eighteen years). The idiosyncratic attitude of this husband-and-wife design team blends English wit and whimsy with a freewheeling historical sensibility. There is something of the circus about this bohemian pair.

The Bannermans' first major commission in their own right was the restoration of the Pulhamite grottoes at Waddesdon for Lord Rothschild, and in recent years they have worked for the Earl and Countess of Arundel at Arundel Castle (the 'Collector Earl's Garden') and the Marquess of Cholmondeley at Houghton Hall, as well as for the Prince of Wales at Highgrove. They are best known for their grottoes, ruins, roothouses, cascades and other architectural features broadly drawn from the eighteenth-century garden vocabulary, though all are given a contemporary spin – Bannerman work never looks like straightforward restoration or re-creation: it always yells out its contemporary provenance, which is another strength. Green oak is a favourite material, used not just for structures and ornaments but also for incidental purposes such as edging. The Bannermans say they like the way the wood ages and silvers so that it comes to resemble stone – though eventually it starts to crack apart in imitation of the artfully faded grandeur that their clients tend to crave as the presiding tone of their demesnes, palpable newness still being infra dig in sections of British society.

The couple met in Edinburgh the early 1980s, when Isabel was a student and Julian owned a bar and was a regular collaborator with avant-garde gallerist Richard de Marco. Their joint garden education began during the

OPPOSITE A level platform of lawn thrusts into the countryside, its horizontal power emphasized by the lack of adornment.
ABOVE Architectural features in green oak – such as this pedimented and obelisked gateway in eighteenth-century style – are an integral part of the Bannerman signature.

245

course of their restoration of The Ivy, an early eighteenth-century Baroque house near Chippenham which Julian was trying to keep going while also running his bar business in Scotland. The couple then moved permanently down south, with Isabel initially working for an interior designer in Bath before their first big project together in 1987, a collaboration with grotto specialist Simon Verity. 'Simon was a neighbour and we went off on a sort of ashram for grotto-makers, living in a cottage on the estate at Leeds Castle [in Kent] for six or seven months,' Isabel recalls. It was after that she decided to go in for gardening professionally, attending horticultural college in Wiltshire and then embarking on the business partnership with Julian. 'We began as grotto-makers,' she says. 'It has taken us a long time to throw off that tag.'

In 1993 they bought the run-down house and 10-hectare/25-acre estate of Hanham Court, in the flicker of green countryside midway between the cities of Bath and Bristol. 'We came here and I have to say I just didn't get it at all,' Isabel recalls. 'There was no garden except for the back lawn. The views we have now were completely obscured. It was really grisly. But Julian saw.'

What Julian saw was the sheer drama of the site, with the potential for revealing fine vistas down to the Avon and beyond from the massive terrace on which the house is sited, the legacy of the monks who built Hanham in the fifteenth century. Tree clearance duly revealed this flat rectangle raised up above two combes served by ancient monastic culverts. The best views are in fact back towards the house and garden as it crests a landscape of diagonals formed by

The house is a mix of styles around a medieval core, set like a ship in a sea of surrounding fields.

a series of steep little hills, like a ship on an ocean. The house is a bit of everything: the medieval core including a fifteenth-century church and gateway, Georgian sash windows across one wing, plus a 'Frankenstein Gothic' (as Isabel puts it) tower and other additions from the nineteenth century. There is also a magnificent medieval tithe barn.

The 0.8-hectare/2-acre garden presented a blank canvas. Now sentinel yew topiaries line the lawn, behind which are several garden rooms all done up in the Bannerman exuberant signature style. These are reached via a wide pathway, the Obelisk Garden, which runs across the front of the house and adjacent church, where vast lime-green euphorbias (*E. characias*), kniphofias and *Iris pallida* erupt from gravel paths, flanked by tall, thin

yew topiaries (dubbed 'flasks') and seats underplanted with box. Masses of tulips appear here in spring, while in the fragrant summer hinterland behind the evergreen topiaries pink shrub roses are a dominant note, alongside delphiniums, peonies and sweet peas. Everything is lush, blowsy and romantic, with nothing of the Continental rigour of the New Perennials drifting style, which one suspects the Bannermans would think of as embarrassingly overdesigned. This path terminates in a gate in the garden's boundary wall shaded by a venerable walnut tree, which opens into the pastureland beyond, with meadow plants (fritillaries, narcissus, humble cow parsley) enlivening the undulating greensward.

An enclosed swimming pool garden can be discovered flanking the lawn, a still space filled with the scents of honeysuckle, lilies and heliotropes, as well as the roses which are so pleasantly ubiquitous at Hanham. (One should never decry ubiquity in roses.)

OPPOSITE The Obelisk Garden of topiaries runs against the front of the house and adjacent church. It is emblazoned with colourful tulips in spring.

BELOW Strong shapes near the house, provided by architectural detail and (as here) topiary, contrast with the swelling countryside around.

OVERLEAF Looking back towards the house across the pasture which surrounds the estate. A treehouse ensconced in a yew tree can be glimpsed to the right.

On one side of this little garden, focused on a simple rectangular pool with more ornamental than amenity appeal, is a chunkily decorated pavilion or grotto in green oak, smothered in white 'Rambling Rector' rose. The decorously pockmarked limestone walls are also adorned with fragments of architectural salvage, much of it with an ecclesiastical air. A typical Hanham scene consists of strong plantings – cardoons and foxgloves, for example – with a backdrop of roses festooning the corner of some intriguing piece of ancient masonry. The Bannermans' style may be romantic, but it is never weedy.

OPPOSITE Romantic shrub and rambling roses are a strong feature of any Bannerman garden. Here striped *Rosa* 'Ferdinand Pichard' takes centre stage.

ABOVE The blowsy roses are complemented by self-seeding foxgloves in white and pink, a look the Bannermans championed for years before it was taken up by others in the mid-2000s.

The swimming pool garden is a reworked Edwardian Italianate pool garden, with roses, pots and salvaged architectural masonry creating the good-humoured Bannerman flavour of fantasy Gothicism.

There is a completely different atmosphere down in the dell area on the other side of the central raised lawn, overhung by huge copper beeches. Here the Bannermans have been able to pursue their interest in magnolias – a tree which apparently none of their clients like – and ferns, which can be enjoyed in great profusion along with martagon lilies, Solomon's seal and cyclamen. The overall feel down here is late-eighteenth-century Picturesque. A late addition to this area is typically arresting: a Neptune fountain consisting of a stepped cascade flanked by twin stumperies. The figure of Neptune, mesmerized and mesmerizing, sits within. The main fountain jet is topped by a metal crown which (in theory) bobbles away at the top all day long.

And that is where the Bannermans continue to be situated in their chosen profession: bobbling along at the top.

OPPOSITE A rocky cascade has been melded with a stumpery in this typically exuberant confection, in one of the monastic culverts that runs to the side of the main garden. ABOVE In this area the Bannermans have been able to pursue their interest in shrubs, small trees and spring bulbs.

Tilbury Hall
George Carter

A MONG modern garden designers, George Carter has a very distinctive presence. His highly stylized and immaculately finished gardens are replete with references to seventeenth- and eighteenth-century design, but somehow this never descends into historical pastiche. Such stylistic eclecticism means that Carter's *oeuvre* could potentially be bracketed with the postmodern movement of the 1980s (when he began his career). Yet his work does not suffer from the dated feel of architectural postmodernism, perhaps because he uses traditional materials in preference to slick and shiny modern finishes.

Notwithstanding the 1980s backdrop, Carter is one of a very small number of contemporary British garden designers who continue in the tradition of the sometimes whimsical but always glamorous formality found in the work of 1930s architects/designers such as Clough Williams-Ellis and Oliver Hill. He trained in fine art (sculpture) and began his work in the gardens world making architectural installations at the 1980s garden festivals in Glasgow and Gateshead. In 1988 he struck out on his own as a designer, making furniture, trellis and objects for garden settings. Gradually he found himself designing the spaces around these objects, until he became a fully fledged garden designer. Chiefly because of his idiosyncratic approach to ornament and garden architecture, he has acquired a reputation for witty and cleverly weighted formal gardens where evidence of his hand is immediately apparent.

The garden at Tilbury Hall dissolves into informality in its outer reaches, though elements such as the urn positioned by the lake, the pleached hornbeams and the twin pavilions remind us that this garden has been designed with precision.

One of Carter's most ambitious recent projects in this mode is at Tilbury Hall, where a garden of neo-rococo exuberance has been carved out of a quiet pocket of otherwise austere countryside on the Suffolk–Essex border.

George Carter first came to the notice of the owners of Tilbury Hall in 1998 through his association with the Romantic Garden Nursery, a Norfolk establishment which specializes in the topiary which has always been a key element of his design signature. Since then the garden has taken shape in piecemeal fashion, which has not been to its detriment because this is a garden of enclosed and discrete parts. Carter has nevertheless managed to create a sense of movement and easy continuity between the different garden spaces, ensuring that gilded bursts of bravura performance are mingled with passages of more low-key enjoyment.

Tilbury Hall is first recorded in the 1320s as an estate in the ownership of the de Vere family, and part of the house is believed to date from the late fourteenth century. Centuries of architectural change have resulted in a delightfully asymmetrical building that sits in an unusual position towards the bottom of a fairly steep hillside, with a small lake to the west – probably the remnant of medieval fishponds – and the red-brick tower of the village church across meadows to the east. When the current owners moved in, the drive came right up to the house; this was removed and the main entrance reoriented on the opposite (east) side of the house. This was just the start: a considerable amount of earth-moving was needed in order to make a garden (let alone a formal garden) viable here, but it was achieved successfully, effectively providing a blank canvas for the designer.

As a formalist, George Carter's instinct was to impose some sense of order on the house through its setting, so he created four distinct garden areas, each of strong structural form, for each of its four faces. To the south is a smooth rectangular croquet lawn, with a Jan Sweeney sculpture of jumping hares forming a fine endpiece, bracketed to the west by a substantial wooden pergola, covered in roses, that links the house with an ancient barn and sympathetic new peg-tiled and clapboard outbuildings that act as garaging.

A new formal canal in the Dutch late seventeenth-century tradition is a rarity indeed in English gardens, but introduced at scale and with conviction, as here, it can seem a perfectly natural adornment.

To the east is the new entrance, set – unusually but rather charmingly – in a corner where two wings of the house meet. To dignify and define this area Carter suggested a range of lead planters against the walls, planted seasonally, and a turning circle for cars round a simple circular pool. From here there is a fine vista across meadowland towards the church tower, the view framed by terracotta urns and animated at ground level by Carter's signature ornament: a replica of the classical Calydonian boar. To one side of the meadow is a thatched rustic hut, crowned by antlers, which Carter designed to house a carved wooden sculpture evoking deer.

On the west side of the house – in place of the old entrance drive – is a parterre of low box hedges, lavender and other greyish perennials, plus black and white tulips in season. This gives on to a lawn terminated by twin pavilions in the Hidcote manner, and beyond a John Cheere statue ('The Haymaker'). There is even a stilt hedge (of hornbeam), though in contrast to Hidcote it extends on either side of the pavilions rather than in front of them, successfully deluding the eye that this is a level piece of ground. A south-facing spring border hugs the wall to one side of the lawn, and here as elsewhere Carter relies principally on evergreen shapes as definition – phillyrea is the professed favourite, though sarcococca is also much in evidence.

A more watery and informal area ranges widely across the southern end of the estate: a stream garden with an 1820s feel (Carter is an enthusiast for Humphry Repton),

ABOVE The garden has a
strong structure but retains
an open feel because few of
its spaces are hedged around.
Features such as the twin
pavilions and the pleached
hornbeams, on the west side
of the house, create strong
boundaries without blocking
sight lines.

OPPOSITE Carter is a master at
managing hierarchies of scale.
Here, a little formal plat by
the house leads south to the
canal and pavilion at its far
end. Vital elements include
the urn, which marks a staging
post, and the expanse of
grass, which acts as a divider.

featuring meandering paths, shrub roses, willows to shelter under and several bridges to cross, including a metal one in seaside blue over the lake. The many changes in level and orientation between these distinct garden areas have been exquisitely managed.

Perhaps the most successful part of the Tilbury Hall garden is the walled kitchen garden to the south-west. This was conceived in part in tribute to Villandry, the celebrated twentieth-century recreation of a classical potager in the Loire Valley, but here Carter has lent his own special touch in the form of substantial wooden frame surrounds for the beds, mulberry-festooned arches, a central fruit cage and other details, all realized in a low-key, grey-blue paint wash. The 1990s craze for potagers led to some rather dinky and insubstantial experiments, but Carter does not fall into that trap here, citing the seventeenth-century Dutch designer Vredeman de Vries as his inspiration for the chunky woodwork which dominates the scene. The owners are frequent visitors to the Far East, and on one such trip they saw a potential double use for wicker chicken coops as cloches or plant covers; these now dot the beds to good effect. For the far, western end of the walled garden, Carter has designed a delightful Regency Gothic camellia house, done in light pink plaster.

One of George Carter's skills as a designer is an ability to create a genuine sense of landscape in a relatively modest acreage – even in town gardens. At Tilbury Hall he has created a feeling of the landscape park with additions uphill to the south of the house,

BELOW The south part
of the garden consists of
several *allées* and enclosures
surrounded by hornbeam and
yew. Bold decisions have been
made with the ornament, to
good effect.

OPPOSITE Cross vistas are
important in the south garden;
Carter is in his element with
this kind of approach.

where geometric structure is created by straight lines of clipped yew and hornbeam hedges. From a specially positioned, hornbeam-surrounded seat against the south front of the house, there is a vista past standard roses, across the croquet lawn and up a long, black, stepped canal to a small banqueting house that incorporates a pair of sumptuous gilded doors from Thailand. This is lit at night to dramatic effect. Adjacent to the canal is a narrower *allée*, flanked by classical pedestals of mottled Hornton stone that looks well against the yew hedge. These are topped by elaborate bronze horns.

Beyond the next hedge is a swimming pool garden, with a large modern conservatory and a jaunty pool house designed in the spirit of the Royal Pavilion at Brighton. Cross vistas bisect this most formal part of the garden, one terminating in a decorative wrought-iron gate with open fields beyond – a very Clough Williams-Ellis touch, as Carter acknowledges – and another in an antique glorietta set in young woodland.

Carter synthesizes the parkland look with a highly individual style which he is happy to admit owes more to Repton than it does to Brown, incorporating as it does formal interventions such as statuary, buildings, avenues of trees, canals and other water features. 'Quite a lot of the jobs I have are about imposing some sort of geometry on the site,' Carter notes. 'To start with, it's nice if your house can be at the centre of the estate, though it hardly ever is.'

LEFT The pergola at the front
of the house, which gives on
to the service buildings, was
conceived as a large-scale
feature in keeping with the
rest of the design.
RIGHT Carter designed the
charming camellia house
in the walled garden in a
Regency spirit. The chunky
woodwork in the beds was
inspired by the seventeenth-
century designer Vredeman
de Vries.

Carter is also one of relatively few garden designers who are able to manipulate and utilize the sky itself. The eighteenth-century French painter François Boucher once observed that nature is 'too green and badly lit'. Part of what he was getting at is the importance of composition in design, coupled with the need for light to be understood as an artistic material in its own right. In landscape design this implies, among other things, the designer's relationship with the sky. André Le Nôtre was perhaps the greatest exponent of this: at Versailles the figurative sculpture acts as a conduit between earth and sky (or cosmos). George Carter, in this spirit, harnesses the big skies of East Anglia for his own ends.

This is a garden of numerous set-piece effects which come tantalizingly close to going over the top, but Carter is an eminently careful designer: the exuberance never topples into extravagance. The garden is subtly interconnected and no part is ever entirely enclosed, so it is possible to wend your way through each region in a relaxed manner.

The pool garden has a distinctly 1930s feel, though the pool house is decidedly eclectic: in form it looks like a Wyatville orangery crossed with the Royal Pavilion, while the fenestration gives it a modern air.

Gresgarth
Arabella Lennox-Boyd

ARABELLA LENNOX-BOYD is not quite what she
seems as a garden designer. Brought up in a
large country house just outside Rome, she
married Sir Mark Lennox-Boyd in 1974 and moved to
Lancashire in 1979 when he was elected Conservative MP
for Morecambe; he served for eighteen years. Over that
period she established herself as one of Britain's leading
garden designers (as opposed to landscape architects –
even though she was qualified in that area) at a time when
garden design was a nascent profession.

Arabella Lennox-Boyd's design style is generally
described as an amalgam of Italian and English influences
– the English for the planting, the Italian for the spatial
– but that is both a lazy and an inaccurate formulation.
The feel of her gardens in England is overwhelmingly
English, with a strong emphasis on herbaceous planting
and shrub roses, topiary in the Arts and Crafts tradition
and a general air of horticultural experimentation. The
spatial awareness is there in the form of her confidence and
skill with architectural detailing and the management of
physical space. This is something which could perhaps be
ascribed to her Italian heritage but might have more to do
with her own talent and professional training, including an
influence which is admittedly slightly more prosaic than the
Roman Campagna: Thames Polytechnic. This institution
(now the University of Greenwich) is where she studied.

Garden designers of the generation immediately
preceding hers – which included such luminaries as
Sylvia Crowe and Brenda Colvin – were barely able to

The double herbaceous border, against the background of the
pleasingly complex gothicized entrance front of the house. The
border is realized in classic style, with campanulas, delphiniums,
nepetas and roses, pointed by the odd contemporary note, such
as spikes of eremurus.

be garden designers at all, because in the straitened post-war atmosphere there was little domestic work to be had. They turned, instead, to the public sphere, designing reservoirs, motorways, coalmines and new towns, which in most cases suited their leftish political stance. Arabella Lennox-Boyd was among the new generation of garden designers to emerge in the 1970s and 1980s, just as it was becoming established as a profession distinct from landscape architecture.

Over the years, she has built up a blue-chip list of private clients, including the Duke of Westminster, members of the Rothschild family and the pop star Sting. Though her social connections may initially have helped, her success is, however, much less about 'who you know' than 'what you know', because she has repeatedly proven herself to be eminently comfortable working creatively at an estate scale, while retaining a feeling of intimacy and floral extravagance in enclosed garden areas. This is an unusual combination in Britain. In country house circles there is a strong tradition of planting advice being given on an amateur or semi-professional basis (that is, people may be paid, but the money does not get talked about, and everything is easy over dinner), which is precisely how Norah Lindsay worked in the 1920s. One drawback of this tradition is that gardens either tend to be designed piecemeal by many hands over many years, or else are simply left undesigned, in terms of the physical landscape (enclosures, steps, terraces and so on). The other option is to employ a landscape designer or architect, who might be able to remodel a large garden effectively in terms of its structure, but will not always be able to contribute herbaceous and shrub plantings which exhibit the charm or sensuous hedonism (depending on how you look at it) which comes from experience and interest in planting design for its own sake. Arabella Lennox-Boyd has both these capabilites, as evinced at gardens such as Eaton Hall, Ascott (the private terraces by the house) and her own demesne of Gresgarth, which – as her experimental laboratory – is the most intensively worked of them all.

She is candid about the practical horticultural problems inherent at Gresgrath. The 3.5-hectare/9-acre site is tucked away at the edge of the Lune Valley, in an elongated bowl formed of three steep and wooded banks, creating the double whammy of wind tunnel and frost pocket. 'Gresgarth is not an easy garden, and for me it was by no means love at first sight,' she writes. 'The house stands on the edge of the Artle Beck, a river that is frequently in spate: it runs from moorland, through several miles of semi-ancient woodland, into the garden. Steep hills, wooded mainly with oak, ash and beech, rise beyond the river and on three sides.' The furious, freezing west wind blows like a gale down the valley; and there is a great deal of rain, adding to the generally watery feel of the place. When the Lennox-Boyds arrived, the park in the valley bottom was choked with the weed-like *Rhododendron ponticum* and past-their-best conifers. The walled garden, on the hillside to the south-west, was planted with Christmas trees and infested with weeds.

But there was potential. The character of Gresgarth is strongly defined by the river which cuts a dramatic swathe through the property, coming into the garden at the eastern perimeter and running in a straight line before performing a right-angle turn and flowing past the east front of the house, perched above. Not many gardens have such a powerful intrinsic element. There was a pond in the lawn to the south of the house and Arabella Lennox-Boyd decided to enlarge it considerably, so that today it could almost be called a lake. 'When we first arrived the pool had no impact on the landscape and looked rather dull,' she recalls. This still piece of water now acts like a domesticated version of the wild river, psychologically balancing it so that it becomes possible to relax in the garden's spaces. There is a slightly Oriental feel to the pond, with a flowering cherry (*Prunus* 'Taihaku') overhanging it, and the addition of a large boulder is a nod to Japanese *shakkei* traditions. But the decisive visual role played by the pond is the way it balances the strident facade of the house, remodelled in 1810 from a medieval core along rather ecclesiastical lines, with tall and narrow (and handsome) Gothic windows spanning two storeys and a dramatic gable at the east end topped by a cross. This fenestration creates pleasing reflections in the water and accentuates the already strident verticals.

RIGHT Marsh orchids and other wild flowers thrive in the boggy ground south of the house, where an existing pond was enlarged to complement the ship-like demeanour of the house.
OVERLEAF The Tibetan poppy (*Meconopsis*) glows amidst *Darmera peltata* and wild garlic around the stream south-east of the house, where the garden stretches on down the valley and becomes essentially an arboretum.

The house appears almost like a gothicized version of that astonishing ship-like garden Isola Bella, which rises up from the waters of Lake Maggiore in Italy.

As Arabella Lennox-Boyd comments: 'After the hilltop home of my Italian childhood, with views stretching for miles in every direction, I found the idea of being at the bottom of an enclosed valley very oppressive. The rugged informality of the landscape posed an additional challenge: my natural inclination is towards symmetry, and it was clearly going to be difficult to impose symmetry here.' The enlarged pond creates a strong sense of place at Gresgarth, imposing its stillness on the landscape and imparting a kind of symmetry by means of reflection. It was perhaps her chief strategy against the incipient chaos of the Lancashire landscape.

But how to make a garden of it? There is a steep drop and not much space between the house and the pond, so she deployed the classic Italian trick, terracing. In this case there is room only for a small, intimate terrace at the upper level, linked via flanking staircases – inspired by those made by Lutyens at Great Dixter – to a more generous lower terrace with chequerboard paving which has the character of a quayside. These linked spaces have a strongly architectural feel which is accentuated by geometrically clipped box shapes at the corners and standard lollipops of *Prunus lusitanica*, but all around are soft plantings of roses (including 'Yvonne Rabier' – 'the only white shrub rose I can grow successfully'), campanulas, alliums, thalictrums and clematis. Flanking wooden arbours at water level are festooned with rose 'Rambling Rector'. *Nepeta racemosa* 'Walker's Low' – less chunky than some of its fellows – is a favourite companion plant among the roses, along with rosemary, lavender, santolina, tall aconitum and larger shrubs such as choisya, deutzia, philadelphus and cotinus. The roses are chiefly Hybrid Musks, notably 'Buff Beauty', 'Felicia', 'Penelope' and 'Wilhelm'. These plantings are hardly revolutionary but they nicely offset the strong design lines at play here – a quality one sees repeatedly in Arabella Lennox-Boyd's garden designs.

The terraces around the house are narrow but well structured, with clipped hedges and topiary, including *Prunus lusitanica* standards, and frothy clumps of bronze fennel and giant alliums rising up to complement the shrub roses.

The east side of the house faces the river as it rushes by, and a similar terraced treatment has been introduced here, though this time the garden spaces are enclosed as opposed to open. A small lawn above the river with yew buttresses and shrub roses at the corners in different colours acts like a miniature quotation of a classic English garden, as if to say, 'We could do this everywhere, but we choose not to.' A 'Chinese' fretwork bridge, set thrillingly high above the water, takes the visitor across the beck and into the watery meadow and parkland beyond, where there are swathes of gunnera, hellebores and ferns, with the bright flowers of iris, primula and meconopsis at the fringes of the river in spring, backed by larger forms of rhododendrons and azaleas. In drier areas wildflower meadow plants have been encouraged, such as oxeye daisies, ranunculus, cranesbill geraniums and orchids. Beyond, the walled kitchen garden has been comprehensively resuscitated, notable features being goblet-trained pears and the beet 'Bull's Blood'

used as edging instead of box. But the main focus in this eastern end of the garden has been on trees – initially the removal of overgrown evergreens (though some fine large sequoiadendrons were left) and the addition of specimens of acers, oaks, stewartias and magnolias. Arabella Lennox-Boyd estimates she has planted more than three thousand trees and shrubs at Gresgarth already, including several avenues (one of liriodendron) and yew hedges which also serve as windbreaks in this sometimes savage environment.

On the other side of the pond, to the west, some strong shapes have been imposed on the garden's ground plan. First, a large roundel of closely mown lawn enclosed by yew, with an old robinia and flowering cherries at the centre. Then a classic double herbaceous border defined by clipped yew hedges, with a kind of entrance vestibule as a prelude and a palate-cleanser at the far end. The prelude takes the form of a fine mosaic garden by Maggie Howarth (who did the dachshund mosaics for Christopher Lloyd at Great

Dixter): pink and grey stones in a swirling pattern with an olive tree emblem (for Arabella) enclosed within a classical portico (representing Sir Mark). An interesting small grass, *Helictotrichon sempervirens*, is grown here at the front of the border: it is a small explosion, neatly defined.

The borders themselves are deep (some 5 metres/16 feet) and well separated by a wide grass path. The grass *Calamagrostis brachytricha* creates a strong rhythm at the back. The borders contain classic cottage flowers such as phlox and veronica, as one would expect, as well as the pleasingly ubiquitous roses, with achilleas and sedums towards the front. Rich hemerocallis lights them up in summer, alongside the red-orange of *Helenium* 'Moerheim Beauty' with, towards the back, the large *Rudbeckia laciniata*. Linking plants in spring and early summer are *Allium hollandicum* 'Purple Sensation' and nepeta, their bulk later replaced by *Geranium* × *magnificum*, with asters producing the main late summer to autumn show.

OPPOSITE East of the house the river flows past below the terraces with their topiary while, beyond, the untidy valley has provided Arabella Lennox-Boyd with an opportunity to grow specimen trees, including exotics such as Japanese maples.

ABOVE From late summer to autumn the borders at Gresgarth are left to stand so that the colours and shapes of the grasses, in particular, can come into their own. Pampas grass (*Cortaderia*) is no pariah here, since this landscape is well able to assimilate its histrionic form.

OVERLEAF In winter the bones of the garden are displayed to advantage: for example, in the way circular structural forms have taken their cue from the amorphous lines of the pool, and the important role played by the native trees along the valley's edge.

Arabella Lennox-Boyd has addressed the topic of the siting of herbaceous borders, which remain the most important showcase of the gardener's art in Britain: 'A herbaceous border can be sited either in the middle distance, making the focus of a pleasant summer walk, or nearer, as a main vista to be viewed from the house.' This is a rather old-fashioned observation – but I mean that as a compliment. It is only old-fashioned because not many garden owners today contemplate the creation of substantial new herbaceous borders in a garden of this scale (Packwood is another example – where the border has been conceived in the 'vista from the house' mode). It rather sums up Arabella Lennox-Boyd's design methodology, in that every constituent part of a garden is considered as part of the whole, with scale understood to be just as important as floral choices; this designer envisages the double border not as a self-contained feature (as it so often is in Britain) but as a feature in the landscape. At the end of the double border there occurs a sort of buffer zone or sorbet between courses: white lollipop alliums thrusting above a mass of *Euphorbia cyparissias*, giving way to the

star grass *Miscanthus sinensis* 'Morning Light' in summer and autumn. This is the classic herbaceous border, with a beginning, a middle and an end.

But this is not a neat landscape. There are some well-ordered episodes within it but the overall feel is of a garden which has been made against the odds. The entrance courtyard does, however, impose a sense of order at the outset, with two octagons of lawn around which the gravel drive sweeps, one enclosed by a yew hedge and the other a fine platform for Gresgarth's Calydonian boar – a fine copy of the iconic Florentine statue of a semi-recumbent wild boar known as Il Porcellino. Gresgarth, it transpires, is Old English for 'Enclosure of the Boar'. And here he is, barely contained – just like this garden as a whole.

A frosted Gresgarth underlines the importance of form above all to this designer – the garden is filled with strong shapes, whether in topiary, paths and paving, hedging or the choice of perennials and grasses.

Bury Court

Piet Oudolf

Christopher Bradley-Hole

THERE ARE TWO quite distinct gardens in the 0.6
hectares/1½ acres of gardened land around this
large farmhouse on top of a ridge in the open
agricultural landscape of northern Hampshire. The first,
behind the house and bounded by various barns and
other outbuildings, is an ornamental garden enclosed on
three sides, on the site of an ex-farmyard. This was the
first garden in Britain designed by Dutch plantsman Piet
Oudolf, and was for several years in the late 1990s a place
of pilgrimage for those interested in cutting-edge planting.
The second, at the front of the house, is a gridded modernist
grass garden with dining pavilion designed by Christopher
Bradley-Hole, which is far less domestic in character than
the rear garden, and subject to more rigorous exposition. It
would be neat to suggest that the two gardens complement
each other, but in reality they are a complete contrast, and
have quite different functions.

John Coke moved in to Bury Court when it was a part of
the family estate, nearby Jenkyn Place (no longer in family
ownership), which itself has a notable garden. He did not
like the house with its messy yards and rather bald and
open setting, and was initially reluctant, but has no regrets
now. He and his wife modernized the house interior and
started a nursery business called Green Farm Plants, which
soon became known as one of the foremost nurseries in
Britain for interesting plants, a place where horticulturally
like minds could meet.

John vividly recalls the day Piet Oudolf came to visit
the nursery in 1986 (when Oudolf was running his own
nursery in Holland). 'I knew it was him at once,' John
says, 'so I went straight up to talk to him. We hit it off
immediately – it was as if there was a chemistry between
us.' Oudolf was a regular visitor thereafter, and it was on
one such visit, almost a decade later, that he and John,
together with Marina Christopher (the plantswoman and

author, who was a partner at the nursery), hatched the plan
for a 'show garden' of nursery plants in the old farmyard
(it opened to the public in 1998). This was an extremely
open and bald space to deal with, where 'a wind is always
blowing', as John puts it, and even now there is a sense that
the plants are hunkering down against the elements. The
resultant scale and emphasis makes Bury Court unusual
for an Oudolf garden: there is a feeling of numerous plants
presented cheek by jowl to create interesting contrasts, as
opposed to the massive swathes of just a few species which
came to characterize his work in the 2000s.

The key decision, however, was not one of plantsmanship
but of materials. The multifarious architecture presented

OPPOSITE The planting of a bare and barren farmhouse yard,
unevenly shaped and open to the elements, was the first British
project undertaken by Dutch plantsman Piet Oudolf. The carefully
composed nature of his earlier work has more recently been
softened by areas with a meadowy feel.
ABOVE Paths of granite setts take off in all directions, as if in
homage to the varied facades of the surrounding buildings.

by the farmyard, and the fact that it is roughly square-shaped but in no way rigidly geometric, called either for a starkly modernist treatment or something more gentle that referred to the agricultural vernacular. The latter course was chosen. The key material is the handsome Belgian granite setts which have been used to make a slightly cambered path taking the visitor to the centre of the garden and then around its edges in an unpredictable manner. The rambling nature of this walkway works well in context and the cobblestones lend a subtle unity to the whole design, alongside the tone of the planting. The distinctive shape of a trio of circular oasthouses overlooking the yard is the other major architectural element, and an attempt was made to reference this by means of a small, tight parterre of spiralling box in one corner.

Cushions and small swirls of clipped box help provide a structure to plantings of perennials and grasses in large beds of amorphous, organic shape. Red and purple flower colour is created by the numerous salvias, valerian, *Dianthus carthusianorum* and *Aster asperulus*, with textural interest added in the form of eryngiums and the fluffy spires of *Persicaria amplexicaulis*. Lower down, some solidity is provided by masses of dark sedums and also Jekyll's old favourite, bergenias. Grasses are used consistently as foils to these more familiar perennial plantings, with the fluffy and full *Deschampsia cespitosa*, for example, playing off the filigree perovskia, and *Stipa gigantea* vying with the orange flower spikes of eremurus (compulsory in the noughties naturalistic garden) as well as accenting splashes of yellow 'sun' plants such as helenium. In the early days the perimeter planting along the eastern, open side of the farmyard felt very much like the showcase moment – almost a long border – but now the rest has grown up to create a balance, and there is a stronger naturalistic element in the shape of several large beds of native meadow grasses mingled with more ornamental subjects. Up at the north end by the barn (which is now used for functions) is a formal pool and a small gravel garden, with sedums, euphorbias, santolinas, sages and eryngiums. This is a remnant of the garden's previous existence as a 'demonstration' space for

A trio of oasthouses inspired the circular, swirly form which unites the garden, in terms of the shapes of the hedges, the beds and the path system. Here, orange eremurus sings out against purple salvias.

the nursery, and not something which would have been planned at this scale under other circumstances.

As a whole, the garden represents the moment when the directive rigour of modernism began to be invaded by the allure of big plantings and naturalistic sensibilities, when traditional English planting design in the romantic cottage tradition began to be challenged. At the time, in the late 1990s (as I recall), Oudolf's new Bury Court plantings of large grasses such as miscanthus, together with big drifts of echinaceas – that quintessential plant of the first phase of New Perennials in Europe – looked radical and new, at a time when plantsmanship in Britain remained in thrall to Arts and Crafts precedent and had reached a peak (or glut) of complexity and sophistication in terms of multiple plant pairings and a supremely pumped-up manifestation of the tapestry tradition of planting design. By the mid-1990s, Edwardian Arts and Crafts had mutated into its rococo phase. There was a

simplicity and strength to Oudolf's new approach, as well as a lack of conventional prettiness and romance, which was extremely refreshing to see at the time.

Something like it was familiar to the well travelled or well read already, in that in the United States James van Sweden and Wolfgang Oehme (OvS) had through the 1980s been practising in a tradition which was similarly derived from German precedent (especially the work of Karl Foerster and his disciples in post-war public parks). But there was still something about this European version of New Perennials which was different. It was partly climate-related, naturally, but it also had something to do with the differing idealized visions of nature on each side of the Atlantic. In America, the prairie dream means that there has always been a great emphasis on showy daisy-like plants such as rudbeckias and echinaceas, used in great drifting masses, while in Europe the palette is likely to be more varied and delicate overall, with far more complexity.

Today Oudolf's Bury Court plantings do not look at all radical or innovative; in fact, it all seems rather dated and also curiously domestic, as John Coke is the first to acknowledge. The sense of domesticity is created by the large number and variety of plants used in the space available. In any case, as Oudolf himself has remarked, the problem with doing anything new is that after five years people start to think it is what they have always done. A good analogy for what has happened is modernist architecture. Pioneering examples of modernism by architects such as Adolf Loos and Berthold Lubetkin have come to seem to be all of a piece with far inferior works completed decades later, and have lost their value as innovative works to all but connoisseurs. The Oudolf garden is today mainly enjoyed as a semi-public space by guests at the weddings held in the large barn, and by the audience which comes to enjoy the Cokes' annual opera production. It never has and does not now have the feel of a private space. For that, John Coke's

OPPOSITE The path system of granite setts accentuates the vernacular atmosphere of the garden, while also imposing a sense of order on its irregular shape. The relative complexity and smaller scale of Oudolf's earlier work can be seen here.
ABOVE The spires of *Ligularia taquetii*.

At the front of the house, facing west, is Christopher Bradley-Hole's gridded grass garden.

horticultual focus has moved to the garden at the front of the house.

Christopher Bradley-Hole designed this gridded garden of grasses with perennials in 2003: twenty square beds laid out in rigorous formation directly in front of the homely tile-hung and red-brick farmhouse, facing west. The combination of geometric formality with naturalistic planting is the hallmark of the designer's work (see Crockmore House, page 112). One 'bed', hard by the tall oak dining pavilion which is the focus of the garden, is a simple black pool that is almost flush with the ground, reflecting the beams of the pavilion and the mature lime trees which overlook the west side of the garden. When one is sitting at the slate table inside the dining pavilion, the surrounding oak structure acts as an ever-changing framing device for the big plantings of grasses and perennials in the beds, with numerous species of miscanthus (notably *M.* × *giganteus*), stipa and panicum,

seven different sanguisorbas, many daisy-like plants (including rudbeckias) and cow parsleys (such as *Selinum wallichianum*), plus thalictrums and the surging spikes of *Eremurus* × *isabellinus* 'Cleopatra' and 'Pinokkio'. *Datisca cannabina*, growing up to 2 metres/7 feet high, is a stand-out plant. The ratio of grasses to flowering perennials has generally been about 70:30, with flower colour restricted to oranges, reds and maroons, though John Coke has recently been moving it even farther towards the grass end of the spectrum. Bradley-Hole has described the referent plant community as a reed bed, the idea being that the detail and variation emerges only on closer examination of a plant range which at first appears almost monochrome. There is a great feeling of luxuriance in this space, the building fulfilling a role somewhat similar to that of the pavilion in the gardens of the Alcazar in Seville, as a restful retreat for refreshment set amidst great beauty. The tall grasses brush against the visitor walking the paths, and there is a feel of being in a maze (despite the fact that the grid is eminently negotiable). 'We wanted it to feel as if you are in a dream-like meadow,' John explains. 'We wanted to use plants which were rather strange in themselves – unusual forms or which flower out of the time you would expect. All to create an other-worldly feel.'

This sense of transcendence is enhanced by the way the grasses and other tall plants sway in the wind, and also by their autumn colour, which gradually melts down into a glorious melange of bronzes, golds and silvers threading through and around each other, offset by the burnished or blackened seed heads and stems of plants which may already have given up the ghost but remain to haunt the garden with their deathly decorum. But the pristine nature of the grid, and the way the beds are each slightly raised and edged with weathered steel, and further bounded by narrow 'ditches' containing gravel aggregate rougher than the compacted material of the paths, create an underlying tone of abstract idealism. The far (west) and south sides of the garden are bounded by geometric arrangements of clipped beech cubes, creating a feel of enclosure, though each cube arrangement has a slot cut through it so that selective views out can be obtained. Bradley-Hole also created a great barn-like garage building out of green oak, to the north, and this is prefaced by a mass of *Calamagrotis* x *acutiflora* 'Karl Foerster'. The success of this simple planting has inspired John to begin another horticultural intervention at Bury Court, in the land to the south of the farmyard. Here he is laying out a large plat of diamond-shaped beds filled only with this grass. If the Oudolf garden represents the 1990s and the Bradley-Hole design the 2000s, perhaps this new area will prove to be a touchstone moment for the 2010s?

The grass garden comprises a grid of twenty square beds ranged around a tall central pavilion, the planting scheme of big grasses and perennials restricted to rich oranges, reds and maroons against a burnished gold and brown backdrop which comes into its own in autumn.

The Laskett
Sir Roy Strong and Julia Trevelyan Oman

THE NAME MEANS 'a strip of land outside the parish'. And the garden created at The Laskett, Herefordshire, by Sir Roy Strong and his late wife Julia Trevelyan Oman has certainly proven to be well 'outside the parish' of both run-of-the-mill horticultural activity and professionalized garden design in Britain. This is a garden that divides opinion radically, its defenders quite as passionate as those who seek to dismiss it. My task with this chapter is to persuade you to take this garden seriously, at least – even if it is not to everyone's taste.

From soon after the time of their arrival on May Day 1973, Strong and Oman were engaged on the gradual creation, as funds and time allowed (for this was a weekend house at the beginning), of a large formal garden of ornamented compartments in the 1.2-hectare/3-acre field adjacent to the Georgian farmhouse. When they bought the house they had not planned, particularly, to make a garden; they only began to think of it when the farmer to whom the field was leased decided he no longer wanted it. The blank canvas was sitting there in front of them. As artists of sensibility, what else could they do?

Strong is a historian and museum director with a particular interest in the English Renaissance period; he went on to curate a groundbreaking exhibition on garden history at the Victoria and Albert Museum (where, during a fourteen-year tenureship, he became its most celebrated director), and to write a string of influential books on garden history. Oman was a theatre- and opera-set designer (having started out in television). The affinity between that discipline and garden design is well established. In retrospect, they look like something of a dream team as the makers of an original and startlingly ambitious garden.

The Laskett is above all an autobiographical garden, quite explicit in its terminology – each area and each feature of the garden has been named after an event or person. Strong has described it as 'the portrait of a marriage, the family we never had or wanted, a unique mnemonic landscape peopled with the ghosts of nearly everyone we have loved, both living and dead'. It's not precisely a portrait of a marriage, perhaps, for the visitor gains no sense of the kind of marriage theirs was – its vicissitudes and foibles, its joys and frustrations. The shade of Vita Sackville-West looms large in twentieth-century English gardening, and perhaps the idea of a 'portrait of a marriage' is a subconscious reference to the title of the memoir written by Sackville-West's son, Nigel Nicolson. The Laskett may perhaps be more accurately described as a commentary on the progression of successful twin careers, and a memorialization of connections, friendships and enthusiasms made along the way.

The garden is an intensively designed series of at least forty compartments, corridors and antechambers, ingeniously crammed into a relatively small space and contained by high yew, leylandii and beech hedges which effectively cut out the rest of the world. As Strong wrote in his memoir of The Laskett: 'Hedges to most people are a burden. To me they are a joy. If I had to simplify The Laskett garden I would indeed sweep away everything and leave just the hedges and topiary. They endow the garden with its romance and mystery, evidence too that a garden is as much about placing human beings in space as are architecture and theatre design. It is not for nothing that I sometimes like to shock an audience by saying to them,

The memorial urn in the Christmas Orchard, an area of The Laskett garden which has become increasingly naturalistic in feel over the years. The urn contains the ashes of Sir Roy Strong's late wife, Julia Trevelyan Oman, and will eventually hold his as well. The inscription from Christina Rossetti reads: ' . . . if you should forget me for a while / And afterwards remember, do not grieve.'

"Remember, flowers are a sign of failure in a garden," a remark that is always guaranteed to produce a reaction.'

The hedge system has facilitated the garden's modus operandi: the element of surprise, a sense of variety enhanced by the many different levels and sloping terrain. This is quite a disorientating garden; being in it is like getting lost in a mansion devised by Lewis Carroll. A series of monuments punctuate the closely linked and variously shaped and sized garden spaces, often in a yellow and blue scheme introduced during the 1990s, which unites the decorative schemes of garden and house. The interpolation of flourishes of colour is reminiscent of Clough Williams-Ellis's decorative use of estate colours at Plas Brondanw (an acknowledged influence), as well as first-hand experience of Baroque gardens in Germany and Eastern Europe, where ornament tends to be painted. Real gold leaf (of the 22-carat variety) is used extensively – perhaps most memorably on the antlers of the *Reclining Stag* statue in the Christmas Orchard.

Given the well-read and well-travelled owners' knowledge of historic gardens, it is no surprise that the garden shows evidence of many and varied influences, from the essentially cellular plan, which derives from the Arts and Crafts tradition and especially Hidcote, to the floral abundance inspired by a defining visit to Arabella Lennox-Boyd's garden at Gresgarth (see page 272), to the gardens of the Italian and English Renaissance, replete with ornament, terracing and stage-set panache. A more domestic kind of influence has come from visits to the gardens of artist John Piper, decorator John Fowler and photographer Cecil Beaton (all of whom are commemorated in the garden). More practical advice flowed as a result of friendships with garden designers including Rosemary Verey – with whom

RIGHT ABOVE The Sundial (from Cecil Beaton's garden), in the Silver Jubilee Garden, looking towards the Rose Garden.
RIGHT BELOW A statue of a gardener, a copy of an eighteenth-century painted figure, presides over the kitchen garden.
OPPOSITE TOP LEFT The *Reclining Stag* with gilded antlers creates a frisson in the Christmas Orchard.
OPPOSITE TOP RIGHT The Ashton Arbour, flanked by painted urns, focused on an antique statue of an unknown king and prefaced by the Parterre (a knot garden).
OPPOSITE BELOW LEFT A painted bear in the Howdah Garden.
OPPOSITE BELOW RIGHT A stone lion holds a shield with 'J' for Julia.

Strong developed a largely good-natured rivalry – and the Dowager Marchioness of Salisbury of Hatfield House. The slightly intense, almost claustrophobic feel to several parts of the garden may be the result of familiarity with the poet and garden-maker Ian Hamilton Finlay's great garden at Little Sparta in Scotland, where the woodland areas perhaps gave Strong and Oman the artistic 'permission' to devise intensively worked passages and twisting walks which can create an atmosphere of almost oppressive circularity. This goes against the conventional design wisdom of recent decades, which is almost entirely founded either on the veneration of the herbaceous border as the *ne plus ultra* of gardening or else on modernist principles of spatial organization. The Laskett garden also owes an explicit debt to Little Sparta for its dependence on inscribed ornament

(most of it by Reg Boulton) – though the approach is rarely allusive here, as it always was for Finlay.

An on-the-page tour of such a complex and varied garden would quickly become wearisome, so I will describe here only some of the highlights, before I try to get to the nub of what the garden is about.

The house at The Laskett has been described by Strong as 'rural Regency of an undistinguished kind', though it is 'pleasing', nevertheless, and 'reminiscent of a small rectory out of a novel by Jane Austen'. Gothic windows and the addition of green trelliswork give what was originally a fairly utilitarian building an airy feel of Regency Gothic, as if the house had been on a day trip to Brighton and come back transformed. It's a look which also places it firmly in the late 1960s and the 1970s, when this retro style was

in the ascendant among the extremely style-conscious. The formal Yew Garden behind the house (to the east) was one of the first garden projects at The Laskett, and was groundbreaking in its day. It is now a parterre of yew (previously box, which was destroyed by blight in the late 1990s, along with much of the box throughout the garden) and clipped amelanchiers. The Howdah Garden to the south of the house features an astonishing metal structure of postmodern aspect, ascended by spiral staircases and overlooking twin fountains and a heather parterre (another original notion). Strong describes this structure merely as a 'viewing point'. This seems at first like a bizarre understatement, given its unique character. But then one realizes that this feature has no symbolic charge associated with the owners, and must therefore be considered chiefly

The Howdah Garden, which is centred on a curious metal structure of postmodern aspect, more interesting to look at than to climb up.

utilitarian, and remain unnamed. Cutting between the Yew and Howdah Gardens is Die Fledermaus Walk, a typical addition at The Laskett in that it commemorates Oman's opera career and also her family history – it terminates in a pinnacle salvaged from that rarefied institution All Souls, Oxford, where both of Oman's grandfathers were fellows.

One of the boldest moves in the garden's structure, and one of the most successful areas today, is the long, straight Elizabeth Tudor Walk which cuts diagonally across the southern edge of the garden. Again, this was one of the first features created, in 1973 (it was originally paired with a Mary Stuart Walk), though, as is the case with various parts of this garden, its form and tone have been completely altered several times. It began as an avenue of poplars, which were replaced by *Nothofagus* and then by pleached lime in three tiers, underplanted with a swagged beech hedge. The straight central path is flanked by a low yew hedge punctuated with holly standards and a staggered row of Irish yew. In a garden filled with small enclosures, sudden incident and constant detail, this long walk, a kaleidoscope of changing evergreen colours and shapes, adds a refreshing element of variety and a relief from unremitting incident. The east end terminates in a crowned and painted column that commemorates two queens, Elizabeth I and Elizabeth II, while the western end contains a memorial-urn monument to Shakespeare – also commemorating the Hamburg Shakespeare Prize awarded to Strong in 1980. As with many such memorials in this garden, it is not entirely clear whether this

OPPOSITE Cross vista into the Yew Garden from Die Fledermaus Walk. In this garden evergreen hedges and topiary are not the supporting cast but the chief horticultural interest.
ABOVE Swags of beech hedge below the pleached limes of the Elizabeth Tudor Walk, looking towards the Diamond Jubilee Urn.

A concatenation of shapes in the Christmas Orchard: a cruciform plan, with a statue of *Britannia* facing the *Reclining Stag* at the far end.

feature is celebrating Shakespeare, chiefly, or Sir Roy Strong, chiefly. Visitors tend to find this either delicious or irritating. Similar difficulties may be stirred by the memorials to pets which the garden embraces, with features such as Sir Muff's Parade (a walk remembering a much-loved cat) taking the pet cemetery tradition to operatic levels.

The heart of the garden, north of the Elizabeth Tudor Walk, contains three principal areas. Nearest the house, to the east, is the Pierpont Morgan Rose Garden, made on a sunken area in the original bare field which Oman thought must have been the site of a tennis court. Previously the only part of the garden to be floriferous (The Laskett has become more so since Oman's death in 2003), it is a paved formal space in the Arts and Crafts spirit populated by shrub roses ('old roses' but also Geoff Hamilton, who no doubt would have been amused to find his eponymous plant in such a high-falutin' garden), low box hedges, frothing *Alchemilla mollis* and colour lower down from *Astrantia* 'Hadspen Blood'. It also contains gilded obelisks, urns, statues, decorative pineapples and a triumphal arch, with beech standards clipped in rounds to help with the overall balance.

The central part of The Laskett's garden is taken up by the cruciform Christmas Orchard, so named because it was first planted with old varieties of apple tree on Christmas Eve 1974. Later, quinces and old pears were added, along with roses, standard wisteria and latterly far more herbaceous perennials of the kind one might see in a 'normal' garden. After Oman's death in 2003, Strong set about revamping the garden, opening it up by removing large numbers of trees (notably overgrown conifers), shrubs and other plant material. Indeed, he opened it up in more ways than one, for these changes were a prelude to the garden opening to the public on a more regular basis. The cross paths and a variety of hedges gradually blurred this area's identity as an orchard and today its character is pleasingly indeterminate, verging on the mysterious (the *Reclining Stag* certainly lends a frisson of mysticism). It is carpeted with blossom from bulbs in the spring.

Against the western perimeter is a concertinaed axis of garden incidents running south to north, starting at the Shakespeare monument at the west end of the Elizabeth Tudor Walk. The visitor turns north to cross the Beaton Bridge into the Birthday Garden (which Sir Roy says 'celebrates both our half-centuries') and on to the Hilliard Garden, named for the great Elizabethan miniaturist, about whom Strong wrote a book. The parterre design (now, post-box, in lonicera) features a 'J' and an 'R'. A few steps farther along, a cross-axis reveals the Ashton Arbour to the left, with urns commemorating the two Ashton ballets Oman designed and to the right Covent Garden, a topiary stage with a cross-axis to the rose garden.

The axis terminates at its northern end in the V&A Temple, an eighteenth-century 'seat' in the Ionic order – inspired by one seen by Strong at Painswick in Gloucestershire – and perhaps the single most impressive

(and restrained) decorative element in the garden, erected in 1988. The inscription in Greek on the entablature translates as 'Memory, Mother of the Muses' – which Strong has described as 'the key to the garden'. It is also a tribute, in its way, to the Warburg Institute in London, which Strong regards as an intellectual wellspring and which has the word 'Mnemosyne' inscribed above its entrance. Mnemosyne was the Greek personification of memory, the mother of the nine Muses – their father being Zeus. Against the back wall is a plaque by Simon Verity with the profile of Strong sandwiched between those of Victoria and Albert; Oman used to say to visitors: 'Victoria's the one without a moustache.'

There is much else to describe but this is where the 'garden tour' ends. 'You had to be there' – that old addendum to a failing anecdote – is pre-eminently true of The Laskett. In real life, the introduction to the garden given in person by Sir Roy Strong himself is an integral part of the 'visitor experience'. This is a garden where the personalities of the creators – and especially that of Sir Roy – loom large at every turn; where every visit is topped and tailed or accompanied by Sir Roy, the garden's impresario, the self-styled 'genius of the place'. Thus the visitor (now able to come on a prebooked tour) has a double whammy of Sir Roy's personality. First there is the man himself, addressing the group, and then the extrapolation, interpretation, interpenetration and triumphal self-examination of that personality and career, as narrated by the garden.

And why on earth not? It's that sort of a garden. As with Vita and Sissinghurst, Sir Roy himself is a large part of the reason why people have come to see the garden – to marvel at the man as well as the place.

However, the relentless autobiographical focus of this garden has proven repugnant to some. They feel that the memorials and inscriptions are boastful and vainglorious. Others find the nooks and crannies, the twists and turns of the garden's structure, its hiatuses and uncertain moments, an affront to 'good design'. The Laskett is a garden which has been attacked more often than perhaps any other in recent decades. I should like to come to its defence.

To the first point, that the garden is self-indulgently autobiographical, one might retort that every good garden is ultimately autobiographical at heart; it is simply the case that this particular theatrically inclined, historically literate couple chose to make no bones about it and put themselves

at centre stage throughout. Yes, it's 'over-the-top' in some ways, but perhaps we need a little more fantasy in gardens; perhaps contemporary pieties about 'naturalistic planting' need a little leavening. Those who criticize the garden for its egotism can have little or no understanding of garden history, which is as much a tale of personalities, dynasties and politicking as it is of horticulture or topics such as the colour-theming of borders or ecologically correct 'wildlife gardening'. Such people are unlikely to have read Strong's academic works, including his pioneering books on garden-history topics such as *The Renaissance Garden in England* (1979), and will therefore have no understanding of his standing as a scholar. They also need to find a sense of humour. There is more than a little self-mockery about The Laskett, and about Sir Roy's shtick in general. And, finally, let's remember that it was Strong and Oman's own garden, made in private and primarily for private consumption. They were at liberty to do what they liked with it.

Perhaps in the end Sir Roy and his wife were simply being more honest than most garden-makers. This garden, as an expression and imprint of the relationship between two people, is certainly more life-affirming than the situation one finds in many gardens, which is that one half of the couple clearly has a more rewarding relationship with their garden than they have with their partner. In the end, gardens are all about relationships – with plants, with objects, with people, with places, and with the garden itself as a whole. It is perfectly possible to forge a deeply felt alliance with a plot of land gardened over years, a place which uncannily appears to have a mind of its own, a place which not only provides a daily 'dialogue' but also requires regular physical interaction. Hands in the soil are an embrace of sorts. A garden can be the ideal place to commune. That strange truth is proven by The Laskett. For Strong and Oman, the garden was an affirmation of their relationship as opposed to an escape from it. As the

inscription on the Triumphal Arch in the rose garden has it: 'Conditor Horti Felicitatis Auctor' – 'They Who Plant a Garden, Plant Happiness'.

As for the second point, regarding 'good design' – well. People who talk about 'rules' of design tend not to be very good designers themselves. Spatial organization is not the be-all and end-all of good design, especially in a situation where tone, character and texture are as important as they are at The Laskett. As long as a garden is authentic on its own terms, surely it can be made to behave as the owner wishes? If this garden seems overstuffed with objects, we might reflect on the fact that the creators of the garden have lived their lives in and through objects, in both their material guise and via their symbolic and historic power. It was therefore the most natural thing in the world – the *least* pretentious thing – for them to create a garden filled with objects and memorials which brim with personal emotional resonances. And in any case, where else can you

OPPOSITE The arms of Edward I, a fragment from the waterfront of the medieval Palace of Westminster, secreted in a niche in the Christmas Orchard.

ABOVE The V&A Temple, commemorating Sir Roy Strong's directorship of London's Victoria and Albert Museum.

see something quite like this? Surely it's far better to be original in a garden than . . . than almost anything at all, in the fraught, authoritarian, conformist and class-conscious world of British horticulture.

Yes, social class is another topic which needs to be confronted here – as Strong himself does. Born in Edmonton, north London, into a lower-middle-class milieu, educated at grammar school and then at London University (not Oxford or Cambridge, like most he has dealt with professionally), Strong has been condescended to throughout his career, and not least in the matter of his garden. The self-referential tone and memorializing impulse of The Laskett garden is seen as slightly embarrassing. The insistence on recording and even celebrating the cost (often surprisingly low) of specific

features is also viewed by some as beyond the pale. Several of the features have been somewhat disarmingly named after the event which enabled the owners to pay for the feature: the Pierpont Morgan Rose Garden, for example (funded by a 1974 lecture series at that institution), or the Beaton Bridge, paid for by the proceeds of a 1988 book about the photographer's portraits. Of course such infra dig references are deliberate on Strong's part – as they were on the part of Oman, who came from a more socially elevated background but one with an intellectual and artistic bent, taking delight in outraging self-proclaimed purveyors of 'good taste'. But it seems likely that it is just this fear of bourgeois knick-knackery which has been at play in the National Trust's hesitancy in considering The Laskett as a property which might be passed on to them after Strong's

death. However, there are strong arguments in favour of the Trust's accepting The Laskett. Garden visitors love to learn about the personalities of those who made the place, and to get to know the garden through them – as, pre-eminently, at Sackville-West's Sissinghurst, the National Trust's most popular garden. The Laskett certainly fits the bill in this respect: Strong has loomed large in the national consciousness for decades; the garden is of considerable historical and aesthetic interest; and there is a massive archive inside the house to draw on.

Ultimately the Laskett is a historical artefact of some importance, and the garden is – for most visitors, anyway – highly entertaining. It is to be hoped that these attributes will come to be appreciated, and that the garden will be preserved for posterity.

The Pierpont Morgan Rose Garden, with the Triumphal Arch in the background. This was the first area of the garden to be developed, on the site of what was thought to be an old tennis court.

Wildside
Keith Wiley

TAKE A YOUNG cider apple orchard which is never going to be commercial. Remove the trees so that you are left with a flat field, slightly sloping southwards. Strip off all the soil. Hire a mini-digger. Learn to drive it. Reshape the land by mounding up banks and berms to make dry valleys, bright open areas, damp and boggy patches, sheltered nooks and a pond system. Thereby create a radical new topography specifically designed to provide habitats suited to the plants you most want to grow. (This is what you might call a 'can-do' attitude to gardening.) Then bring all the soil back in, varying the depth – again, to suit particular plants. Add 3,500 different varieties from all around the world, organized in a highly individualistic manner, in emulation of plant communities seen in the wild. Relax?

Of course not. For Keith Wiley, creator of the Wildside garden and nursery in west Devon, remoulding the landscape was just the beginning of the adventure he and his wife, Ros (an artist), began in 2004, when they bought a large plot situated at the bottom of a lane in the village of Buckland Monachorum. The garden he is now creating there, in three distinct parts, is testament to deep horticultural knowledge and also sheer bloody-minded willpower. The fact the couple have achieved all this with no other help and very little money only adds to the sense of wonderment, shading towards awe.

Keith Wiley previously made his name as head gardener, for twenty-five years, at the Garden House, a classic twentieth-century plantsman's garden less than a mile away in the same village. Fiercely independent-minded,

Keith Wiley used a mini-digger to create his new garden on the site of an old cider apple orchard. Paths wind around banks and berms planted with favourite daisy forms and elegant daylilies and dieramas.

through the 1980s he had pioneered at the Garden House a style of gardening which was ahead of the naturalistic curve. The New Perennials movement of Piet Oudolf and others only really became a feature of the British gardening scene from the mid-1990s onwards. Many years before that Keith Wiley was making naturalistic garden areas or environments redolent of the South African Cape or California dunes, evoking the tonal qualities of plant communities found in nature. As he says, 'Over the last twenty years I have been totally convinced by the concept of taking gardening ideas from natural landscapes.' (One might replace the word 'convinced' in that sentence with 'obsessed'.) It's true that Beth Chatto was also thinking along these lines in the 1970s and 1980s, but her Essex garden was always domestic in feel; Keith Wiley, by contrast, had ambitions to create a garden that would actually look and feel like the wild.

As a result of his early and continuing experiments in this vein, Wiley has built a reputation as something of a prophet shouting in the wilderness – an identity one suspects he rather enjoys, despite protestations to the contrary. Some of his claims for what he calls 'Wild West, seat-of-your-pants, pioneering gardening' can come across as rather overblown. For example, in his 2004 book, *Wild Side*, he states that 'we have all but ignored the biggest single source of gardening ideas on the whole planet – the countryside around us.' Any knowledge of garden history would disabuse one of that idea – look at Gertrude Jekyll, for example, all of whose work was inspired by the natural world, as was that of her contemporary William Robinson. But one takes the point in that the 'colour-theming' of borders – with little regard to combinations found in the wild – had become the aim of most serious gardeners in Britain through the 1970s and 1980s, when Keith Wiley was developing his ideas. His work is certainly a long way away from Rosemary Verey's, for example.

The first bit of Wildside that Wiley attacked with his mini-digger was a 0.6-hectare/1½-acre plot of earth which he contorted into naturalistic shapes borne of close observation of topographies in nature. 'I have always felt', he states, 'that if I can make my garden look good and sit comfortably in its setting before a single plant is put in the ground, then I am already halfway to success.' Most experienced gardeners think about soil seriously, and will even replace it wholesale if they find it mitigating against

good horticulture, but very few would contemplate such radical interventions into the shape of the land. For Keith Wiley, however, this is at the heart of gardening, not least because the shape of the land 'speaks' to us in a direct way. 'People get very emotional looking at a big landscape view,' he says. 'It's that sort of emotion you can tap into in gardening – it's very powerful.' So while he admits to being initially attracted by the flowers and colour, 'in my case it is the overall composition and structure of the view that stir deeper feelings of well-being. It is this latter response, which I am sure is present subconsciously in many of us, that is almost entirely ignored in our gardens.' He eulogizes the qualities of randomness in nature – the way, for example, paths on heathland seem to meander rather aimlessly, 'changing direction suddenly as if created by some drunken sheep' – and he tries to replicate this by means of his own delvings with the digger.

The larger banks of the Wileys' new landscape are home to shrubs and small trees, including hydrangeas, eucryphias, magnolias and many different kinds of acer, most of the latter grown for their spring (rather than autumn) foliage. The height of the banks even creates effective areas of shade on the northern sides. But the overall character is that of a rocky landscape: another strong conviction bubbling up from Keith Wiley's conversation and writings is that plants look their best in this kind of environment. This notion appears to have had its genesis in his earliest plant-hunting trips, to rocky Crete in particular (he talks passionately about the hairs-on-the-back-of-the-neck moments of seeing plants in the wild – it is this he wants to recreate 'at home'). The plants in such places need sun, so light levels were another key consideration. The majority of the Garden House was north-facing, whereas Wildside faces south with an extremely open aspect – Keith Wiley has called the site 'a festival of lights'.

Walking the canyons and narrow paths, even now one has a sense of being surrounded by encroaching plant life.

RIGHT Wiley's philosophy of naturalistic planting favours an impressionistic botanical approach to plant communities seen in the wild, which means that Japanese acers can sit happily with South African kniphofias and classic cottage-garden plants.
OVERLEAF At Wildside the scene is naturalistic in theme but far richer than anything in the wild – this is a supercharged vision of nature which gives the plantings an almost psychedelic flavour.

Keith Wiley points out that one of his tricks was to build the banks up high and place plants along the tops of ridges, to increase their apparent size and therefore one's overall impression of the age of the garden. Daisy forms such as anthemis abound on the lower slopes of the banks, while choice plants including the elegant grass *Eragrostis curvula* and delicate-flowered rhodohypoxis pop up at regular intervals. The New Zealand spruce *Dacrydium franklinii* is a notable specimen. Of the bulbs, agapanthus and erythroniums are probably the stars, planted in generous swathes in emulation of their distribution in the wild. There is a dramatic sense in this garden of moving from one episode to the next – an impression of wildness, but always an underlying awareness that the scene is manmade.

Key to Wiley's philosophy is the notion that plants deserve to be appreciated in their own right, without preconceptions – 'I don't like to pigeonhole plants,' he says. So he grows 'cottagey' plants like wallflowers, campanulas, pinks and lavender in 'non-cottagey' ways (halfway up a bank, for example) and rehabilitates 'over-domesticated' shrubs such as hebes and euphorbias into 'wilderness' settings, as if to give them back their self-respect. Keith Wiley is sceptical about the ornamental aspects of the New Perennials movement, which he sees as another chapter in the continuum of border design which began with Jekyll. He makes a distinction between his own work and that of Oudolf. 'I was coming at it from the wild, starting from that end of the spectrum. Piet and the others were taking what existed [that is, the herbaceous border tradition] and making it looser. I think that style is narrow and limited.' Another element of his philosophy is mimicry: he favours 'exotic' trees, for example, which are similar in habit to the vegetation surrounding the garden. In the case of Devon he claims that magnolias echo sweet chestnuts, all birches remind us of native birch, witch hazels are like the native hazel, and so on. He even argues that maples, far from simply yelling 'Japan!', are redolent also of native hawthorn.

Then there are Keith Wiley's pet obsessions. At the bottom of the newly dug landscape is a pond area with a refined Japanese feel, where the key vista terminates in a group of Brewer's weeping spruce, which he recalls growing from seed some thirty years ago. Just above here, a group of wisteria have been treated as free-standing shrubs, each one growing into a different shape, to arresting effect; Wiley calls it his 'wood' of wisteria. Generally speaking, he likes to plant more rather than less of particular plants, partly, he says, because that is how one tends to see plants in the wild – in large, complementary groupings. His emphasis is always on the accurate observation of nature, enumerating 'the overall balance of trees to shrubs, perennials and grasses; the balance of sunlight to shade; the general topography and undulations of the land itself; the colour and texture of the ground's surface; the colours and textures of the plants and the combinations, colours and shapes of any flowers.' Some of this seems to be stating the obvious but the obvious is rarely stated with such precision. He adds: 'Occasionally these features, or leitmotifs, are almost instantly apparent to you and at other times they may gradually insinuate themselves into your consciousness.'

Self-seeding is discouraged in this garden (unlike at the Garden House) but an illusion of it is created by means of the use of linking plants which crop up throughout – these include the maples (mainly *Acer palmatum* varieties), dieramas in spring, miscanthus, calamagrostis and stipa grasses, asters in autumn and hemerocallis. 'I've always used link plants,' Wiley observes, 'mainly to create a consistency of form, not colour.' He particularly values the calamagrostis and stipa for their ability to keep back weeds. With the addition of thousands of other plants – many of them disarmingly common – the result is a super-naturalistic jewel-box of a garden with almost hallucinogenic qualities, especially when, on a good day, it is all lit up by the sun. When he arrived at Wildside, Wiley says, 'we were plant-rich but we didn't have any money': key to the success of the venture has been the re-establishment of the existing Garden House nursery at the new site – including all the plant stock, which Wiley owned. Refugees are also welcomed: to populate the garden he also took in abandoned plant material from other nurseries, including leggy cercidyphyllums and some odd-shaped magnolias.

The courtyard garden can be found on the other side of the polytunnels used to grow nursery plants. Created in 2009, this is a large cruciform walled garden with a wisteria-clad pergola along one side. The light-coloured stonework is a conscious echo of the sandstone Wiley

A series of pools linked by a stream can be found at the far, lowest end of the garden, where unfashionable plants such as colourful astilbes are used with abandon. This area comes dangerously close to feeling domesticated.

saw in Bryce Canyon, Utah, on one of his treks, as well as adobe walls. The recipe here was 30 tons of dungheap, 250 tons of topsoil, with a gravel topping (though Wiley insists it is not a 'gravel garden'). The space is packed with plants, as one might expect, everything from mingling groups of pink gaura and red *Gladiolus* 'Ruby', through

ferns and epimediums, spiky yuccas and sea kale, to giant specimens of *Hydrangea aspera* Villosa Group and clumps of grass-like restios. *Melianthus major* is in evidence, but instead of being selfconsciously placed as an 'architectural plant', as it so often is, it is integrated. 'There are no prima donnas here,' Wiley observes. This was previously a nursery

stockyard and the old windbreaks have been left in place to create some vertical emphasis. As it is, there are completely different vistas to be enjoyed from different spots, just a few metres apart from each other. The colour palette is quite limited in specific areas, though ultimately the range is wide.

The courtyard garden introduces a new note, with a feel midway between the Mediterranean and New Mexico, with English Arts and Crafts features such as the long pergola thrown in. But the emphasis again is on the plants. Here, yuccas and dahlias in the foreground vie with kniphofias, hemerocallis and a structural underlay of bulky grasses.

ABOVE Even Christopher Lloyd in his pomp at Great Dixter never attempted colour combinations (or car crashes) of the scale and outrageousness seen at Wildside. What other English garden dares to place fluorescent yellow kniphofias against electrifying purple catmint?

OPPOSITE, CLOCKWISE FROM TOP LEFT *Eryngium* x *zabelii* 'Forncett Ultra' growing amidst *Centaurea triumfettii* subsp. *cana* 'Rosea'; *Dierama* 'Wildside' (a cross made at Wildside between *D. dracomontanum* and *D. pulcherrimum*); *Gaura lindheimeri* 'Rosyjane" in front of a pot holding *Verbena* 'Homestead Purple', with *Lychnis coronaria* and white-flowered *Olearia* 'Waikariensis' behind; *Geranium* 'Buckland Beauty' and *Allium schmitzii* with *Anthemis tinctoria* dwarf form in the background.

When I asked Keith Wiley about the repeated use of nepeta, his reply was revealing: 'I've always loved bluebell woods.' If this sounds somewhat oblique, he continued: 'You can't see bluebells in our garden. But catmint is the same colour as a bluebell wood. You can create the effect of bluebells without using the anti-social plant itself.' For Wiley, in order to honour a plant community which has found its niche in the gardener's memory, it is not necessary to replicate exactly what is found in the wild (and here he diverges from the Sheffield School), as long as the general tone is honoured. 'I don't want to copy what I see in a prairie,' he asserts. 'I want to take the feeling I get from a prairie and then recreate it.' (This is precisely what the High Line in New York was supposed to do, incidentally, but signally did not.) It's what you might call 'associative planting design', in that he associates certain forms and colours with particular natural habitats and plant communities, and has these in mind when planning areas of the garden. 'If you

see plant associations in the wild,' he says, 'you might not know what they are, but you can recreate the effect.' It's an extrapolatory technique. This attitude can be linked to the tradition of the original 'wild gardener', William Robinson, the contemporary of Gertrude Jekyll who was perhaps even more influential on the ground. Robinson enjoined gardeners to garden in a naturalistic manner – particularly in woodland and at woodland edges – using plants from all over the world, including 'exotics', just as long as they seemed to sit happily in the scene. Wiley's attitude is similar, in that 'anything goes' in his garden, provided it pleases the plantsman-explorer's eye and has an authentic ring. It really doesn't matter if your Western Australian garden has South African Cape plants in it.

The ambition does not end at the walled garden. Beyond it is a quarry area created with the mini-digger on an even larger scale – at perhaps twice the size of his earlier forays. There is even a natural swimming pond complete with a sand 'beach' tucked into its folds. Birches and pines have been planted on the ridges, while the use of bulbous plants such as agapanthus and crocosmia is even more wild and naturalistic than elsewhere, as they are left to array themselves across the steep rocky slopes. 'Agapanthus plants in an area like this are a completely different proposition from when they are squeezed into a herbaceous border,' Wiley says. Kniphofias and sedums also crop up in groups, with drifting asters continuing the colour into autumn. Previously Keith Wiley rued the way Lionel Fortescue, creator of the garden at Garden House, filled in the quarry on the estate. Perhaps Wiley's new venture down the lane is one way of righting that perceived wrong. He has certainly made a garden now which he can call entirely his own.

The grasses are beginning to come into their own; in time the fluffy stipas will thicken and the gaps will be filled by burgeoning perennial plantings. But it is the shape of the land which ultimately gives this garden much of its personality – nothing like this could have been achieved on the original flat site.

Index

Acknowledgments

First of all, thank you to all the garden owners, custodians, gardeners and designers who collaborated on this book, providing access, information and guided tours.

I would like to thank Andrew Lawson for agreeing to work on the book, and for producing such a definitive survey of these gardens with his customary acuity and panache. Big thanks, too, to Jane Sebire and Rachel Warne for their first-class photographic contributions, which enrich the book.

Jo Christian, who commissioned the book and has seen it through to press, has been patient, wise and good-humoured throughout the process; once again it has been a pleasure and privilege to work with such a skilled and experienced editor. The designs of Anne Wilson are of the very first order, sensitive to the rhythm and nuance of the text as well as the feel of the picture sets. With regard to the text itself, I would like to thank Tony Lord for checking the botanical accuracy of text and captions, and also for creating a superb index.